WILD METRICS

ALSO BY KEN EDWARDS

Verse
Good Science, 1992
eight + six, 2003
No Public Language: Selected Poems 1975-95, 2006
Bird Migration in the 21st Century, 2006
Songbook, 2009

Prose
Futures, 1998
Bardo, 2011
Down With Beauty, 2013
Country Life, 2015
a book with no name, 2016

WILD METRICS

A POEM

KEN EDWARDS

grand
IOTA

Published by
grandIOTA

2 Shoreline, St Margaret's Rd, St Leonards TN37 6FB
&
37 Downsway, North Woodingdean, Brighton BN2 6BD

www.grandiota.co.uk

First edition 2019
Copyright © Ken Edwards, 2019. All rights reserved.

Typesetting & book design by Reality Street

A catalogue record for this book is available from the British Library

ISBN: 978-1-874400-74-5

This is essentially a work of imagination.
Names, characters and places have a complex relation to real people
and locations, and incidents narrated may not necessarily have
occurred in the way or in the sequence described, or at all.
Apologies for any confusion created.

This book is for all those people in my life, living and dead, whose fictional avatars figure in this narrative, and for many more who do not appear.

Also for Brian Marley, whose help and advice with writing I appreciate.

And especially with love for Elaine, who has been an essential presence for the past two decades and more.

The project / The process   7

Winging it   71

Lower Green Farm   135

A nest full of eggs   191

The project / The process

It was not a farm at all, despite the name. It was a five-bedroom, two-storey house set in a huge, rambling and overgrown garden off an unmade lane off a semi-busy thoroughfare in an outer London commuter suburb. Pratt's Bottom was just down the road; how they all, K's friends, tittered at that. In the other direction were conventional bungalows and semi-detached dwellings laid out in neatly circumscribed estates, housing neatly circumscribed lives. Across the main road and beyond an undistinguished patch of green where people walked their dogs was a block of Thirties-Elizabethan buildings enfolding a laundrette, a newsagent, an ironmonger's, an Indian restaurant.

But this house had been condemned. And it had been offered to them (that is, to K and his friends, or if not his friends, any person or persons he might persuade to reside with him) for an unspecified period.

The only photograph I have of it, four decades later, is the one that is on the cover of one of my books. A book I barely remember. It is out of print now. There was poetry in it. The monochrome photo is of the frontage, and has been magnified to the extent that the black and white dots of the printer's screen are fully visible. You have to stand a distance from the book, opened out so that back and front covers can be seen as a spread, to discern the image as a whole. The frontage is very wide, surmounted by a great wedge of pantiled roof. Two bedroom windows are visible in the shade of the eaves, and two ground-floor windows on the right. Left would be the front door, but it is completely shrouded in dark grey: represented as a cluster of tiny white dots separated by larger black spaces, or alternatively large black dots surrounded by tiny white spaces, signifying impenetrable shadow. You can just make out, though, the paler form of one of the Italianate columns that hold up the portico in front of the door. From the appearance of the surrounding (monochrome) shrubbery, the photo would seem to have been taken in spring or summer.

Lower Green Farm had been condemned because it was right in the path of the proposed route of the M25, London's new orbital road, which was due to be built in the following few years, once all the compulsory purchases, permissions and demolitions had been completed. This K and his friends needed to understand, should they agree to take on the property. In return for a thirty pounds weekly fee, there would be issued to them (by the local council, via the Patchwork Housing Association) an open-ended licence to occupy, which could be revoked at any time.

They were not told who had lived there previously nor when it had been vacated by its former owners, nor whether it had ever actually been a farm. They didn't ask.

•

Memories are fractal: the more you focus in and magnify them, the more self-similar structures appear in their interstices, that is, in the gaps between them; and then magnifying those further reveals the even more remotely embedded memories in between them that were hitherto inaccessible. And as these in turn emerge, you wonder whether this process is infinite, or would be infinite were it not for physical constraints that are as yet unknown to us. But in the meantime those memories continue to arise in a kind of stream of particles, of shapes anyway, moving in unpredictable ways, carrying with them their meanings or imagined meanings, their echoes of desires or imagined desires. There are rhythms associated with this process and it may be the case that the interlocking rhythms are all that it signifies and all that will remain of it. Who knows? Who knows anything? There are hints in the narrative that follows, which might be termed a thought experiment, that may provide partial answers. But you do not want to be left in a stupor with negative outlines, you have to make something. You make something of it, and it has to not matter for the time being at least whether that something has what might be termed authenticity, because, also, nobody can determine what *that* is.

•

Write what you know, he was advised. But he had already concluded he didn't really know anything. And he certainly didn't know what he was doing. How could he? Therefore he could only write out of ignorance. He wrote pages and pages of stuff generated out of this ignorance, this unknowingness. When he read these pages back, decades later, they seemed vaguely familiar.

•

Fine weather was breaking up into fine rain, thunder and lightning not far off now. As evening came on, the streets were deserted except for one or two shiny parked cars, observed through a screen of rain-needles shot through with a peculiar and very exciting amber light. The pub was shut. Pale blue and pink patches appeared in the sky to the west, but it was dark overhead. This contrasted with the white glare of the desk lamp. As he wrote, pounding the keys of the Olivetti, he heard children's voices coming and going outside.

•

Henning the Dane who worked in the Patchwork Housing Association office in Ladbroke Grove had told K there was this "beautiful" house outside London available now for five years. Or up to five years. It could be as little as six months, though. You never could tell when it came to local authorities and lawyers and planners. Technically, the purview of the London Borough of Bromley, but yes, unusually, outside London. Patchwork was offering it *pro tem* to anyone who wanted to set up a community there.

Henning was placid, long-haired, ginger-eyelashed, doubly denimed. K, who had cycled into the office to do a day or two's typing to eke out his benefit, had said he was interested. It was chance that brought this about: Richard who he used to share a house with had phoned him to tip him off. It was nice hearing Richard's voice again: Hell-llo Kkkkk ... how are yoooo? Uh, I thought yoooo'd uh like to knnnnOW Pppppp-atchwork nnneeeed ssssomoneto doooosome adadadmin coz ssssomone's off ssssick.

Of course, K no longer lived in a Patchwork shared house, but he was having problems in the flat off Westbourne Grove he had moved to. The gas supply had been cut off because the landlady, Mrs J, had not paid the bill, and consequently (although she had provided him with an electric kettle and a calor gas stove for the time being) K was withholding his rent. It was a stalemate.

K said he would think about it. He was confused. On the one hand, he'd had a vision of an artistic community, where people would be free to pursue their imagination and its fruits. On the other hand, he had left the Share house in Sunderland Terrace after two years – following his two-month sojourn in the States, on tour with the Rock Star – because he couldn't stand communal living any longer (he didn't tell Henning this, obviously). And that was why he was currently on his own in the flat off Westbourne Grove. On the third hand, he was now possibly going to be evicted from that flat. On the fourth hand – outside London? no way.

K told Henning he was going through a "mixed" time with the girl he had met last year (on the rebound from Marie), whose name was Lynne, and had had a "bad, weird" weekend. He had just received a hand-made postcard from her featuring one of her delicate water-colour washes, urging him not to be "alone with his grief". What the hell was that supposed to mean? In a previous letter she had quoted Krishnamurti saying the followers of Zen were "doomed". She was at her parents' farm in Hampshire now, shortly to go to Spain for a month with her best friend. He was listening to Albert Ayler in his flat, and also the spine-chilling voice of the Chilean singer Violeta Parra, a favourite of Lynne's. He had been reading Beckett (*Texts for Nothing*), Gerard de Nerval (*Journey to the Orient*), Julio Cortázar (*All Fires the Fire*), Gertrude Stein (*Three Lives*), Freud (*Psychopathology of Everyday Life*) and Harry Mathews (*The Sinking of the Odradek Stadium*).

As he listened, Henning nodded sympathetically in his

gentle Danish-hippie way. They had gone on to talk of other things. They had discussed the strange experience they discovered both had shared of remembering a previous dream within a dream, and concluded that such "memories" were probably fake.

•

Women had been attracted to K but then gone off him, which he found puzzling. Naturally disposed to melancholy, he had dark curly hair and during this time was starting to experiment with a vestigial moustache. A sort of white Jimi Hendrix effect was the idea. His speech was fairly RP with traces of what later became known as Estuary, but there was something not quite right about him. Once or twice, when his ethnic origin had been revealed the comment had been "Ah, so *that* explains it" (or something to that effect). Lynne had probably wanted him to be more Hispanic; that was why *she* went off him eventually and took up with a real Spaniard. Or perhaps she had at first liked the idea of a poet, as a romantic ideal – that often happened – then went off him because her idea of a poet and his did not in the final analysis match. They had agreed about Lorca, but she didn't like Ginsberg and had never heard of Olson, much less Tom Raworth, Lee Harwood or Roy Fisher, and didn't seem interested in finding out.

•

Eighteen months prior to this, K was to be found with his bicycle, trying to gain entrance to the Rock Star's discreetly salubrious home in an exclusive London neighbourhood. He could see a carmine baby Rolls Royce parked in the driveway beyond the railings. He'd rung the bell at the front gate several times but there had been no response. Fortunately, a man appeared on his bike, who turned out to be the gardener, and let him in. And the housekeeper, who had a strong London accent, greeted him at the door, confirmed that he did have an appointment for 11.30, said he could leave the bike in the front hall.

Tea was served in the dining room, in proper china cups and saucers. They sat round an enormous polished wooden table. On one wall was an original Magritte, on another a framed gold disc. Maybe even platinum. In one corner an abstract chromed-metal sculpture, possibly by Paolozzi, in another corner a harmonium, in a third a huge classic American jukebox carrying a stock of old rock'n'roll and contemporary reggae 45s.

The Rock Star and his wife entered the room. As is often the case with famous people, he looked smaller in real life. They all sat round the table. The Rock Star fired a question at K: What's seven times five? K said: Thirty-five, last time I checked. Right, said the Rock Star with a knowing grin. It was his idea of a joke to break the ice, evidently.

The meeting was about the Rock Star's thirteen-year-old step-child, Buttercup, who wasn't present (she would have been at school that morning). The girl was falling behind in her lessons, principally because she was repeatedly being pulled out of school to go on tour with her parents, and the head teacher had put her foot down and said if this happened again she would have to exclude her permanently. So her parents would have to hire a tutor for the forthcoming American tour. That would satisfy the head teacher. The head teacher was a friend of the self-styled "educational therapist" John W, to whom as it happened Buttercup was being sent weekly for "treatment" – basically, cramming. John W divided his time between work with disadvantaged kids, often *pro bono*, and tending to the children of the rich, for which he charged mightily substantial fees. Now Buttercup's head teacher had appealed to him in her hunt for a tutor. It was a bit of a problem. The role required a qualified teacher, but anyone who fitted the bill would likely be in the midst of the school term and unlikely to want to give up their job for an engagement of no more than two or three months. And so one morning he had turned to K, who happened to be in the office doing that day's admin. You've got a PGCE, haven't you? he said. K had indeed acquired a teaching qualification three years previously, but had decided pretty soon that teaching was the last thing he wanted to do. It would be a doddle, John W had said, nodding seriously. Buttercup just needed a little remedial work in English and maths. But, but, K protested, although his lead subject for his postgraduate teaching diploma had been English, he had not done any maths since O level. *Remedial* maths, said John W. It seems Buttercup, despite having entered her teens, was academically at the level of a seven-year-old. It would be a doddle, he repeated reassuringly. I can give you the text books, he said.

That was why K was here.

He sat across the table from the Rock Star and his wife, while the housekeeper moved in and out of the room carrying teacups and milk jugs. She returned with a plate of bacon and egg, which she set before the Rock Star, who took up his knife and fork and munched in between pleasantries.

After the times-table volley there were no more searching questions. It was clear neither the Rock Star nor his wife could think of anything more to ask. At no time did they ask him about his previous experience. Had they probed, they would have found that K had never actually taught any children since teaching practice during his postgraduate year. He had been offered and accepted a job in a comprehensive school starting in the September after he was due to graduate, but in July had had a panic attack and phoned the school to withdraw. The school had threatened to report him for this – the timetabling had already been done, so that was a fuck-up as far as they were concerned – and since then it had been unclear whether his PGCE was in any meaningful sense valid. He was probably on some government black-list of unreliables.

Buttercup and her school prowess or lack of it were not mentioned again that morning. K complimented the Rock Star on his magnificent jukebox and on the choice of reggae records inhabiting it, and the Rock Star beamed proudly while continuing to pick at the bacon and egg. K was careful, though, not to sound like a fan, and steered clear of the Rock Star's own recording and performing history; and that in retrospect seemed a good decision. The Rock Star's wife, who had interjected a comment from time to time, flicking a strand of blonde hair out of her eyes, said K would need to report to the tour management office in Soho to "sort out all the details". Neither actually offered the job in so many words, but it was heavily implied that the deal was done.

On the way back, K, in a state of great excitement, called in at the Kypriano restaurant in Chalk Farm where Marie was working to tell her all about it. By then, things were not great between him and Marie. They had lived together a year, sharing a room in Sunderland Terrace, but she had now moved into another room, and he rarely saw her because she was working all hours at the restaurant. So the conversation was guarded. But she said she was pleased for him. Her arm was bandaged, he noticed. She had fallen downstairs at work, she said. It was nothing to worry about. He noticed, not for the first time, that whenever she talked about the goings-on at the restaurant she unconsciously lapsed into a cod-Greek accent.

•

Lynne was at the party, but she was avoiding him, probably dancing with the Spaniard now. Anyway, he hadn't seen her since the start of the evening. He was a bit drunk, a bit stoned. It was all a bit sweaty. He knew scarcely anybody. His sister was in there somewhere too, with the man who was to become her second husband. He cheered up somewhat when the reggae came on the sound system. *Exy-duss*, chanted Bob Marley; it was his latest. *Movement of Jah people*. Killer bass line. The long version, good. The totality of creation was there, evident for all to feel, the beautiful ligatures of conscious music.

•

But he was on the rebound from Marie, after all. K had met Marie over two and a half years earlier at John W's office, where he had a part-time administrative job at a pound an hour. The outfit was called The Hampstead Centre for Continuing Education, though it was situated nowhere near Hampstead but in this shabbyish terraced house, down the road from the Patchwork shared house in Sunderland Terrace where K then lived. Where the shabbiness quotient was high. Both were short-life houses licensed through Patchwork. It was believed John W had social ties with the Patchwork founders. And an offset litho printing machine was installed in one room of the premises, which was the official Patchwork printer, used to manufacture letterheading and other official literature. K had his eye on this for possible poetry publishing purposes, if he could only learn how to use it – a cut above his Roneo duplicator.

Marie was also doing bits of administration and filing, in her case in return for her "treatment", which in effect meant John W helping her with her O levels. John W was kindly and droll. He always wore a grey three-piece suit, and his trimmed grey beard and glinting glasses made him look like Freud, especially when he reclined in his professional leather chair. He was lean, almost cadaverous, and suffered from a "bad back", hence could never stoop to pick up anything hefty, or indeed anything at all, even a book that had fallen to the floor.

K's first impression of Marie had been that she was rather sweet and also full of energy. Dark-haired, with a pale complexion, full lips, chubby fingers. She was nineteen years old. He knew that she had had a troubled history, because John W had alluded to this in his guarded way.

The office was only a short walk from Sunderland Terrace. So to get to work K didn't even need his bike, which remained parked in the gloomy entrance hall of the Share house. It was cash in hand, two days a week. That was sixteen pounds. Pretty convenient for allowing him to write, without hassle from the SS. Also helpful as a distraction from the internal politics of the community house, which although officially having adopted a collective approach to decision-making, with weekly house meetings and all, was actually run by K's friends Des and June. They it was who had made the initial approach to Patchwork with a proposal for a shared house – called Share – in which able-bodied and disabled people could live together equally; for June worked for a national disability charity and had had a vision of the future. And so this five-storey short-life house (if you counted the basement – though Sean lived separately on his own down there with Dennis the Magic Dog) had been procured on licence from Kensington & Chelsea council. Thus far, however, no actual disabled people were in evidence.

Des was jovial, bearded, prematurely avuncular. He called himself Professor Chaos, or something like that. That was a sort of stage name. Referred to himself as a "hippie Jew". An early adopter of green politics, non-violent, communitarian, a visionary. Always had something to say, mostly in jest. If he was misunderstood, he would come out apologetically with a saying quoted from one of his uncles from London's East End: "I speak three languages: English, Yiddish and Rubbish." He was a performer – had done some acting, was a friend of the comedian Mel Smith. One of his party tricks was talking nonsense syllables very rapidly in a Russian accent, perhaps imitating another uncle. He had set himself up with a workshop on the ground floor of the partially rehabilitated Sunderland Terrace house, where he recycled furniture, machinery, packaging, timber offcuts and other detritus that he found in skips or scrounged from exhibitions at Earl's Court or Olympia and brought home in his dilapidated Transit van. K's Roneo duplicator, on which he ran off poetry pamphlets, was parked in a corner of Des's workshop.

June was warm and amusing, always reading books and not reluctant to make pronouncements on them – K was impressed by her grand dismissal of Graham Greene as "one of those mediocre English writers" – and a little older than Des. She loved to wear a hat. And she loved Des, and shared his politics. But was more sceptical, maybe. Occasionally she would come out with a killer sardonic comment, in a Birmingham accent, after he had held forth for a bit. She was a psychologist by profession.

Des and June had recruited K to this scheme of theirs, persuading him to abandon his dogsbody job at an independent publisher in Holland Park, the one he'd fallen into when he abandoned the teaching profession, and to live off the SS for a year while writing and helping do up the house. They took him to visit the founding father and guru of Patchwork, Greg Moore, who lived at the top of one of the many short-life houses licensed by Patchwork in the borough of Kensington & Chelsea. He was an old Etonian who had seen the light. He was rumoured to have once been a monk. He knew the playwright Heathcote Williams, who lived in a squat nearby. Previously, Des had called in on Heathcote Williams about some later abandoned theatrical project, and taken K with him because he had expressed interest in meeting him. Heathcote Williams had perfected the white Jimi Hendrix look to a degree K couldn't have matched. All K remembered afterwards was him standing in his kitchen passing a hand through his wild hair, ranting about something.

So there lay Greg Moore on a huge mattress on the bare floorboards of this top-floor room, while Des, June and K sat on cushions which formed the only other furniture. A joss-stick burned in a holder on the floor. He seemed to have forgotten what he had convened the meeting for, instead talking at length about a canoe tour of America he was planning. Greg Moore had long hair, was dressed in jeans and a tie-dyed T-shirt, his feet bare, and talked in a low, mellifluous voice. When he stood up to go across the room for a book or some other thing, it became obvious he was very tall. Other Patchwork people quietly came and went all the while. A short-haired man, dressed bizarrely in a dark suit and tie, popped his head round the bedroom door and greeted Greg Moore with a warm handshake, and the two discussed a legal question for a minute or so. While they were talking, June whispered that she recognised him as a member of the House of Lords.

As Greg Moore returned to the bed to recline again, apologising for the intrusion, K suddenly noticed something: he appeared to have only four toes on each large, bony foot. K lost the thread of the conversation thereafter as he counted and re-counted the toes: big toe, one, two, three, big toe, one two, three.

Two years later, Greg Moore would be killed in a car crash in Wales along with his lady. That would send shock waves through Patchwork.

•

For a while, the household consisted only of Des, June and K. A regular visitor and intermittent resident was Bode, a bearded South African whom Des and June had known when they were squatting in Bristol, and whom they regarded as something of a teacher. He looked like Solzhenitsyn. He had campaigned against apartheid, and as a result was now apparently *persona non grata* in his native land. Bode rode everywhere on a Honda 90 motor-bike. He was said to have a wife and children in Dover, and his relationship with them was obscure. K conversed long into the night with Bode. He talked about keeping a journal and how difficult it was to make it reflect what was going on in his head; it seemed either to degenerate into a trivial day-to-day account of events or to become vaguely philosophical and inflated, but in both cases "reality" remained outside it. He speculated whether he ought to write down fantasies and things he knew to be totally untrue, and whether that would paradoxically nudge the journal further towards a semblance of authenticity.

Bode spoke at length about the necessity and difficulty of living in the moment. He called that Process. He was sceptical about scientific objectivity. He said if in the Middle Ages you were to question the Trinity you would (at best) have been laughed at; today, if you questioned the existence of the atom, which with its proton, electron and neutron was another "three in one" myth, you would get the same reaction. Nevertheless, Bode's heroes were Albert Einstein ("One Stone"), Rudolf Steiner ("Many Stones") and the Lord Jesus Christ. In truth, K did not know what to make of all this. And he was unaware just how it was to turn out, on that night to come when Bode teetered over the edge on which he had been balancing.

But meanwhile Bode was interested in K's poetry, which K had been submitting to various poetry magazines, and collecting for a pamphlet he intended to print on the Roneo with a silk-screened cover by Des. Bode mentioned he had written poetry himself. He showed K a poem of his own – he called it a parable – that had been printed in a South African magazine a few years previously. It was titled "A Little Fantasy":

> The old man said, "Now that you have
> dug up this understanding, see how dry
> the earth is. I search the distant
> peaks for rain clouds."
> I asked him, "Do you think that our
> desire to know ourselves is our undoing?"
> He smiled. "You ask so many questions,"
> he said.

K was intrigued. It had a kind of Zen quality, obviously, but with an African slant. He wanted to see more of Bode's work, for possible use in the magazine he was co-editing with his friend Robert. Bode said he'd dig some stuff out.

•

North Kensington, especially the area bounded to the west by Ladbroke Grove, to the south by Notting Hill Gate and to the east by Paddington, was in flux. Whole streets had been condemned, their properties set in abeyance pending redevelopment, either to be demolished to permit the erection of public housing or to be sold to the new gentry for tarting up. Tall Victorian or Edwardian houses – tired ones, rows of them – had fallen into disrepair, their original owners from generations ago having passed on, their half-lives while divided up as flats or houses in multiple occupation (the ranks of dead doorbell buttons by their front doors testified to this) now almost spent, but the funds to refurbish them as yet unavailable. Every street featured at least one skip by the kerbside, yellow, rusting, continually filled with rubble, bricks, planks, furniture, the remaining legacies of dead residents (battered suitcases spilling memorabilia nobody could find a use for), and also daily household rubbish opportunistically and illegally offloaded. Occasionally a skip would be hitched to a trailer by men in overalls and towed away, but soon another would appear in its place.

What some saw as urban blight others seized as opportunity: squatters moved in here and there, some organised, some political, some as haphazard in their movements and motivations as birds or mice. Most were white; the largely Afro-Caribbean population that had nestled in these parts since the 1950s continued to survive in the interstices and to live their lives and do their jobs somehow. The smell of ganja and the evidence of "culture" was to a great degree prized as exotic by many of the young incomers, especially the college-educated ones, but in truth there was not much real contact. Some of the council estates were still home to traditional white working-class residents, who might or might not have made their peace with the Afro-Caribbeans but would have been largely hostile to the educated incomers. And some of the older white middle-class indigenes hung on in the area too, aghast (if they were owner-occupiers) at how the value of their properties continued to fall, contemplating the awful prospect of selling up at the bottom of the market.

But Patchwork Housing Association had been set up as an honest broker, intervening with the council and private owners, offering a use for dying properties for periods of months or years, until such time as they were ready for permanent resuscitation or for sweeping away. Short-life housing, it was called: licences to occupy, emphatically not permanent tenancies. No guarantees, no long-term futures. Patchwork's shtick was communal living. Every household they licensed had to be committed to this, or at least pay lip service to it. It was squatting in effect, it had a political meaning, that is to say it signified resistance to Power, but it was legal, and because of this Power found it quite convenient.

•

For the first few weeks, there was a great deal of work to do on the Sunderland Terrace house: making secure (some broken windows to be fixed), cleaning, stripping, replastering, painting and decorating. It was not, however, in too bad nick generally.

There was a lot of house there. Four storeys actually. No direct access to the basement, which was Sean's fiefdom. Sean was a squat, pink-faced man, like an over-sized dwarf, with big, chubby fists. After one or two initial encounters, when he shook hands with all the incomers, he was then scarcely to be seen for weeks. He was either in Ireland or in prison, according to who you talked to.

The house had evidently once been very grand, but there were signs of more recent multiple occupation; for instance, a lockable door separated the flight of stairs leading to the top floor, which incorporated its own tiny mezzanine bathroom (though there was no functioning hot water as yet) and three rooms, one with a sink, which might have formed an independent flat. K commandeered the largest of these, which had a magnificent view over the rooftops to the east. The bedrooms on the floors below had dowdy fitted carpets, but this had bare floorboards, and the ceiling sloped. A double mattress had been acquired, and a number of bricks that had been found lying around downstairs, when stacked, supported the planks that were his bookshelves.

A small boy wandered in through the open front door while Des and K were painting the walls of the ground-floor rooms. He seemed happily loopy. Hello, he greeted K. Hello, he greeted Des. Hello, what's your name? said Des, laying down his roller. Ollie Chalk, said the boy. What's that?

He pointed up at a location in the room near the ceiling.

Des said: That's a picture rail.

Picture rail.

He wandered into the other rooms, and they could hear him repeating: Picture rail, picture rail. Then, before he could be stopped, he scampered up the stairs. After a while, he returned. He reported that three rooms upstairs had picture rails but the others did not. He then felt obliged to re-check the ground floor rooms.

They heard a woman's voice on the front steps: Ollie Chalk! Ollie Chalk! Are you in there? She darkened the threshold. Upon which the boy flew into a tantrum and would not move, until inducements by his apologetic mother softened him sufficiently to consent to being led out.

Each day, when he was finished doing painting and decorating in the house, Des retired to his workshop or went on excursions in the van either to carry out small removals for money or to scour the skips of West London for raw materials. The Patchwork workforce were meant to be doing most of the heavy or specialised labour to bring the house into a livable condition – plumbing and electrics – but they were rarely seen, and Des had to nag them. The house smelt of plaster dust and paint. There were ladders everywhere. Autumn was approaching, the evenings were drawing in, the electrics were still not functioning properly, it was dark and cold outside the ambit of the portable electric bar heaters and working lights.

Each day June went off on the tube to work at her office in central London. She did psychological assessments of disabled children and adults to determine their needs. She was talking to her employers about identifying disabled people who might benefit from communal living, but nothing had come of this yet.

Every other day, Ollie Chalk arrived to wander round the house and check out the picture rails. Picture rail, he would say authoritatively, pointing at each one before moving to the next room where he could still be heard muttering to himself.

Eventually, his mother would arrive saying, Time to come home, Ollie Chalk.

Then one day he didn't come, and he was not seen again.

That was the way it was.

•

K did his writing on an Olivetti Dora portable manual typewriter on a rickety table upstairs in his room, sometimes feeding in mimeograph stencils to run off later on the Roneo. He was assembling an issue of the poetry magazine he co-edited with his friend Robert. Sometimes he used the big office typewriter downstairs, the one Des had rescued from a skip. When you hit the carriage return lever, the long carriage slammed to the right with an almighty whump, almost catapulting the heavy machine off the table.

While the hot water was still to be fixed (a problem with the Ascot heaters that had not yet been resolved by the Patchwork workforce), he visited his parents once a week for a bath. From time to time he took lessons from Des in basic practical tasks, for instance, plastering, which he did extremely ineptly – or often helped him with the removals business for a few quid. Once the two of them had to move a piano, which had not been mentioned in advance by the customer, down three flights of stairs. He was signing at the SS, and cashed the resulting Giro at the bank or the local Post Office.

Bode had a room in the house, which he also used for writing in, but was more frequently travelling obsessively on his bike between London, Bristol and Dover. His absences were usually mysterious, and he was rarely available to do practical work. Then he reappeared unpredictably.

What was that poetry magazine, the one you co-edit? asked Bode.

Aardvark, said K, without thinking.

Ah, very South African.

No, actually, that's what we were going to call it. We ended up with *Alembic*.

Bode said that suggested alchemy. Alchemy of the word. He liked that. K suggested he might submit some poetry for the magazine. He said he would, as soon as he was back from Bristol.

More people joined the household, but most of them didn't stay long. A couple who seemed nice at first but didn't participate in the weekly meetings or join the communal meal, became more and more withdrawn, spending most of their time in their room, and eventually disappeared altogether, owing their share of several weeks' rent. They took with them a chest of drawers Des had lent them when they had had nowhere to store their clothes. Des, normally full of benevolent feelings towards the rest of the world, was radically pissed off.

A friend of Des and June's from Bristol, Roger, who had been an architect of living theatre, also stayed for a few weeks, but later decided to return there to be with his kids. Before he left, they had a house party. Someone had scored a substantial piece of dope, and there was beer and wine too. June made some food. One of the rooms in the house was designated the anonymous room, and you had to wear a sack (with eyeholes) over your head when you went in there, but everybody cheated. Bode, Roger and another friend of Bode's who had just been received into the Russian Orthodox church gave a performance of ethnic chanting and bottle-percussion. They were quite drunk and stoned by now (except for Bode, who didn't indulge in drugs, and whose high was purely natural). Then Roger sang an improvised duet with June's stuffed toucan, which had everyone in hysterics.

A nervous cat had attached herself to the household. June fed her, and so she returned frequently. She had had kittens that had died. Her stink filled the kitchen. One sunny morning, she met a tom-cat on the kitchen annexe roof visible from K's bedroom window. Terrified, she arched her back, stiffened her tail, pressed her ears back flat against her head. The tom watched sleepily, unmoving. Then she began to defecate, her hindquarters shivering as she rhythmically deposited turds onto the slates. Finally, she yowled piteously and backed off. The tom turned and disappeared.

Five minutes later, both cats gone forever, a crowd of glistening flies fought greedily over the pile of shit.

For such a large house, the garden was surprisingly perfunctory. It was also in a pitiful state, and nobody volunteered to tidy it up. But there were fruit trees in it. As the winter slowly retreated, spring triggered tiny green, furry fruit on the tree nearest the house, which revealed themselves to be peaches.

Birds sang outside. Inside, on the hi-fi, which was working again, Eric Dolphy played flute.

As K was walking down the road one afternoon, remembering the passage he had read that morning in André Breton's *Nadja* about "significant coincidences", he suddenly conceived the idea of taking a photograph of the household members (such as they were at the time) grouped at the front door, and made a mental note to arrange this. Then, on turning the corner, what did he see immediately but a man taking a picture of a couple standing in front of their house. That evening, he told Bode, who was back from his travels, about this complex coincidence: the Breton passage leading to the symmetry of the thought and the act subsequently witnessed. Bode called it "synchronicity", mentioning Jung. He said he experienced such things all the time. Once, he and June had encountered each other by chance in Oxford Street, just at the instant he was throwing a banana skin in one litter-bin and she an orange peel in another. He recalled the first time he had met K at a local jumble sale. On the way there, in Des's van, Des had been talking to him about K. At that very moment a woman had crossed the road in front of them carrying a dog in either arm; behind her, a third dog. Then, on arriving at the school hall where the sale was taking place, he had seen two dogs leashed at the doorway, one on either side. And inside was K – wearing a T-shirt with a picture of a howling dog. The third dog. K remembered that T-shirt: a black silkscreen image on a light blue background. He didn't have it any more.

This was part of Process, Bode explained, and one had to submit to it, not try to contain or own or explain it. This was a major theme of the book he was writing. K had the impression Bode's book was a doomed attempt to reconcile the irreconcilable. The book was provisionally titled *The Statement* or *A Statement*. Making a statement was for Bode a political commitment, for instance making it clear where you stand on apartheid. But authentic living in Process meant no statement could be definitive because of the implication that all potential had been fulfilled, that there was no more to say. So a statement could only be an affirmation or enactment of one's current state of consciousness.

Des, who had entered the conversation, interrupted excitedly, saying that was Theatre.

K said it was Poetry.

They all agreed that nothing was ever fixed.

•

K wrote: "The mode of being I call living-on-the-planet is the mode of being of the poet. It's impossible to describe, but it has to do with feeling the natural cycles, the rhythms of the planet/body. During the last fifteen months I've learned a lot from my academic friends (for instance, Robert) about structure and methodology, and it's made me more self-conscious, in the best sense of the word, but that's only half the story. I would like to write more open poetry, poetry whose structure is what it says, poetry which enacts in words the living-on-the-planet feeling."

He stared at this for some time. Then he sighed, and crossed it out.

•

Poetry – what the hell was it anyway? There was a time when K thought he knew. But since leaving college, he had kept regular contact with Robert and their mutual friend Peter – they had all been undergraduates together – and they continued to meet in each other's homes – bedsits, furnished flats or short-life houses – to seriously discuss the new stuff that was being written now. And it was a revelation. They read voraciously from poor photocopies: Charles Olson sprawling all over the page, Roy Fisher's oblique explorations of the city, Ed Dorn's insane riffs on Billy the Kid, or whatever. They talked about it. They talked about their own attempts at poetry. K was also writing short stories at the time. Robert and Peter were a little older than him, very measured in their ways, their insights gleaned and codified from patient reading, and already on their way to an academic career, whereas K had semi-flunked, gaining only a lower second, which was a disappointment if the truth be told after all the high hopes, but what the fuck, it was a question of survival now.

And then there was the crew of misfit poets with whom K had drifted into contact, with their wild metrics, they were something else. They were outside the walls. They never analysed, they just did it. K bought *Poetry Information* magazine from Compendium Bookshop in Camden Town, and scanned the listings of other poetry magazines in the back, looking for good fits. He sent a few poems – they may have included the one about Captain Beefheart – to a magazine called *Streetword*, which it turned out actually was sold on the streets by its editor, each issue consisting of a sheaf of mimeographed or photocopied pages, some of non-standard sizes, also including odd-shaped pieces of cardboard with imagery on them, all stapled together somehow. The legendary Jeff Nuttall was among the contributors. And to his surprise, the poems were accepted by Mike Dobbie, the editor, who sent him a very kind letter in return. So that was good.

It was probably at the National Poetry Centre in Earl's Court that he met Mike for the first time face to face and started to have some very useful chats that put him in the alternative poetry picture. And introduced him to the world of small presses; that was new too. Mike was thin, short-haired, somewhat dapper, totally adored David Bowie. The stately Victorian building in which they met housed the Poetry Society, an august yet decrepit body that had been taken over, in a surprisingly well-organised coup, by the exponents of wild metrics and their antecedents and associates and heirs, headed by the likes of Bob Cobbing, the already legendary sound-text poet. And so where the highlights under the previous regime had included such decorous occasions as the national verse-speaking competition, with certificates as prizes, there were now free-ranging events every week, indeed daily: readings by the likes of Roy Fisher, Lee Harwood, Barry MacSweeney, Tom Pickard, who had previously been just names in print to K, public talks and interviews, exhibitions of concrete poetry and suchlike, not to mention a print shop where anybody could go in and learn to print their poems, not to mention copious and well-lubricated conversations about poetry and everything else next door in the White Hart pub, where Glaswegian poet and editor Eddie Linden, lean and grizzled, would haunt the bar, sidling up to customers with his customary chat-up line "D'ye wanna buy a *po'try* magazine?" to which it seemed inadvisable to reply in the negative.

Ah, bliss it was, probably. Mostly.

And there was K's old college mentor, Professor Eric Mottram, interviewing the equally legendary Basil Bunting about North-East dialect in poetry, and Persian ghazals and British espionage in Iran, and whatever. And there were talks about Dada and Surrealism, and debates about whether computers might have a role in composing poetry, and visiting American poets, also already legendary, and the swiftly becoming legendary Bill Griffiths, LOVE and HATE tattooed on his knuckles, Robert-Mitchum-in-*Night-of-the-Hunter*-style, rumoured to have ridden with Hells' Angels and to have killed a member of a rival biker gang, but who was also a scholar of Anglo-Saxon, with a PhD it was said, teaming up with the magnificently eccentric Paula Claire and with Bob Cobbing to give delirious performances of vocal sound-art in virtuosic but insane counterpoint.

And Mike mentioned to K other people he should meet: Allen Fisher, an artist-poet who had worked with Fluxus, he said, a scrappy pamphlet of whose he had published, and Paul Brown, who translated Surrealist verse and organised an essential reading series every week at the Enterprise pub opposite the Roundhouse in Chalk Farm, and there was also David Miller, who it turned out lived quite near him in Notting Hill, an Australian poet who was a friend of the American poet Cid Corman who edited *Origin*, and who knew about Buddhism and free jazz. Enough, or too much, as Blake had declared. After such evenings, K went home, if the half-derelict short-life house he shared could be called that, to meditate on what it all meant, for himself, and for the writing he was trying to do.

•

Three people who did stay with the household for a while were K's other former college friend Keith, his girlfriend Meryl and their friend Phina (short for Seraphina). But Meryl was having treatment for leukaemia and was in the Anaemia Ward in hospital most of the time. She was seriously ill. Keith, caring for her, came and went. Then it was discovered he had to go into hospital himself to have a knee cartilage operation, which didn't help. He was a talented singer-songwriter, and had played with a folk-rock band a couple of years previously that had done John Peel radio sessions but had broken up in acrimony before recording an album. He it was who had first stayed at the flat off Westbourne Grove that K later spent a year in. He it was who had inspired K to acquire a guitar and teach himself a few chords.

Phina, who was tiny and kindly, with baby-blue eyes, brought strange men she had befriended home and had acid trips with them in her room. Once, she gave ten pounds, all the money she had, to a man in the street who claimed to be an American draft-dodger who had nowhere to stay. Another time she went with Des on one of his periodic tours of the local skips for materials, and they came back in the van with a lost soul they had picked up: a young man who had nothing to his name but the clothes he was in, a pound note, and a black-and-white cat he carried everywhere. He had a middle-class accent, and his eyes were permanently glazed behind cracked spectacles. He was frequently unable to finish a sentence. Phina and Des made him a cup of tea and spent several hours talking to him in the kitchen, but he seemed utterly scared and paranoid, questioning everything that was said: What did you mean by that? Did you say turn on *the* radio or turn on *a* radio? Why did you say hello? He asked to go to the toilet, spent ages in there with the light off, and had to be coaxed out. His cat had meanwhile gone to sleep in front of the electric heater. Eventually, around three in the morning, Des gave up and went to bed (June had been asleep since eleven), and

Phina put him in one of the empty bedrooms, where he remained for the rest of the night and did not re-emerge in the morning. At two the following afternoon Des anxiously knocked on the door several times asking if he was all right. He appeared to have barricaded himself in the room with chairs. Eventually, he consented to come out. He mooched around for a while, ate a slice of bread, then picked up the cat, which had been wandering around, and left suddenly.

In the early hours of the following morning, before it was light, the doorbell rang. Des got out of bed and went downstairs. It was the young man again, now minus the cat, asking if he could use the toilet. Des told him politely he could not. He disappeared and, like Ollie Chalk before him, was not seen again.

•

So this was the household Marie joined, when she moved in with K. This did not happen straight away. What happened was that K started looking forward to his Wednesdays working at the Hampstead Centre, because that was the day Marie Palmer came in to do the filing. She cheered him up. The first time he came in on a Wednesday morning she was there already, and introduced herself: Hello, I'm Marie, I do things around here. He ribbed her about that, and she laughed, and afterwards it became a catchphrase between them.

And in the weeks that followed he learned a few more things about her, during those pleasant hours when they worked on either side of the table in John W's office, K doing the ledger, making out the invoices and writing the letters to clients, Marie filing the copies and making the coffee. That her surname, Palmer, was a married name; that she had been married at sixteen (that is, a mere three years ago, K realised), had had a child, a son, immediately after; that the baby boy had been taken away from her (into care? she changed the subject quickly, it was obviously painful – and anyway, neither the whereabouts of the child nor the whereabouts of Mr Palmer, whoever he had been, were necessarily his business). That she did not know who her own parents were, and had been brought up in a succession of children's homes and with foster parents. That John W had taken her under his wing following a referral from the probation service, and was teaching her a great deal, and to great effect, for her evident intelligence had not been served well by her schooling. All this she related seriously over the weeks, but it was as though she was talking about someone else, and she skirted around the reason for being on probation; pretty soon she made a joke, and she was back to being herself again, whoever that might be, at any rate a person with great reserves of joy, which was astonishing in the circumstances.

In response, K talked about himself, and his friends and interests. He described the Share household and how it worked. She wanted to know who all these people were, why they were living together, what they all did. He gave a potted history. She said she was currently sleeping on a friend's sofa; she was really interested in this idea of communal living. He invited her round to meet the household. More people were needed to fill the house and help pay the weekly licence charge to Patchwork.

K and Marie loved each other's company. There was a great gush, a metaphorical one. What it meant was what it did. It was a time of munificence and good fortune.

She introduced joy into his melancholy head. And this joy spread to the spleen and lungs and other vital organs and also outward into the limbs, so that they were all suffused. What a surprise, what a gift.

Marie moved in. She was allocated a room. Des and June liked her. She got on well with Keith, with Phina, and also, when she came out of hospital – in remission from her leukaemia with her hair very short and fluffy – with Meryl.

At this time Bode was no longer an official part of the household, if there was any such status, but he continued to appear from time to time. By then the episode of Bode's freak-out was in the past, and K didn't tell Marie the full story of what had happened; she was wary of Bode nevertheless, having picked up something about it. But Bode did take to her and decided that what she had was good for K, and told them both so. He had been discharged from the mental hospital following his breakdown some months ago, and he was really together now. Really? For a while, everything he said was sensible. He was talking proper sense. Actually, and this was extraordinary, it was Bode who was in some respects the most together of them for a long period, at least while he was there, which was not all the time, guiding the day-to-day and week-to-week functioning of the group, with disciplined weekly household meetings in which the practicalities could be discussed in a coherent way, tensions which might have built up were defused, and the whole thing could move forward. Marie played an enthusiastic part in all this. She had emotional intelligence; she had greater perception of what others were feeling and thinking than K did, for instance, and the things she had to say were often helpful.

She didn't smoke dope, always passing the joint on without a word when it came to her, as did Bode. She had used drugs in the past, she said, and they did not agree with her.

Although Marie had been allocated her own room, the one next to K's – she brought with her only a few black dustbin-bags full of clothes and some books and other possessions in a couple of suitcases, and a mattress to sleep on – she spent more time in K's room, and then, inevitably, in K's bed.

At first it was chaste if delicious cuddling only. Marie said she had been "fitted with a coil" (K was unclear what that meant, other than that it signified a green light of sorts) but was "having her period" (which he did understand by then). But sooner or later – it was sooner, rather than later, to be precise – the relationship progressed. They started to take great delight in each other's bodies as well as each other's mere presence. Marie kept most of her meagre possessions in the room she'd been allocated, but in reality spent most of her time in K's, pretty cosy with the orange shade of the bedside lamp shining on the rows of books on their brick-supported planks, and the acoustic guitar and the typewriter table, and the blue glow of the paraffin heater's pilot light in the middle of the room. When she whispered to K in the dead of night, "I love it when you fuck me," that, he knew, was better even than the actual sex; well, it was more than just a relief. It was better even than that letter inviting K to submit a short story to a series of anthologies of new writing. Nothing could go wrong now.

John W soon found out what was going on. He took K aside. You know Marie has had serious problems in her life? K said he knew. Well, I trust you, said John W. It was a kind of blessing.

Marie received no money from her filing work for John W – it was just a quid pro quo for her O level tuition. She needed a proper job in order to pay her contribution to the household. She did waitressing, that was her thing, and as luck would have it she was offered a job in a Greek restaurant, twenty quid a week plus tips, the disadvantage being that it was in Chalk Farm, which was quite a way, and also it was a late shift, four nights a week finishing at two in the morning, which meant she needed a lift home. But the manager sorted that, no problem. He liked her, she said, because he knew her from before, when she had worked at another restaurant owned by his friend; he knew she was reliable, she would just get on with it.

She would go off to work on the bus at five in the afternoon, thus missing the house communal meal. K tried to do some writing in the late evening, though it was difficult avoiding the something that was always going on in the communal living room, whether it was television or talk and/or a joint being passed around. Anyway, he retired to bed around eleven, read till midnight, switched the bedside light off. Between two-thirty and three in the morning he would be awakened by the soft sound of Marie coming up the stairs and into the darkened room. He always looked forward to that. Sometimes she would have made herself some toast in the kitchen and brought it in. He'd switch the light back on. His parents had given him a coffee percolator for Christmas, and she would fill that and plug it in, and they would have a cup of coffee sitting in bed together on that big mattress under those chocolate-brown sheets. Then eventually they would drift off to sleep in each other's arms. K would be up for breakfast downstairs at about ten, with whoever else was around, while Marie slept on until midday or so.

When the intimacy had established itself, Marie began to reveal a little more. Late one night, in bed, she got very emotional. She started talking about her baby. Her baby had not been taken from her and adopted. He had died. There was a silence. K said gently: How did that happen? Marie said: I don't know. One moment he was alive in my arms. Then he wasn't moving.

There had been an inquest, a court case. The outcome was that she had been put on probation. Nothing had been proved or disproved. The whereabouts of the child's father was not known.

Marie couldn't say any more, and K let her be.

She said that John W had helped her a great deal.

She couldn't talk now, sorry.

Once, Marie had arrived home unusually early. Was anything wrong, worried K. No, she had been chatting to a couple of police officers in the restaurant as she was coming to the end of her shift, and they had offered her a lift home. They had sought to impress her by driving at reckless speed in their squad car along the deserted London streets, on one occasion the wrong way up a one-way street with the siren screaming.

By now, winter had somehow been endured, with its snow, ice and hail up and down the country, though mostly evading North Kensington; spring and then summer came on, hot and dry days alternating with heavy rainstorms. Someone on the radio speculated that the world climate pattern was changing as a result of human interference with nature. The rest of the world was experiencing droughts. Turkey invaded Cyprus (there was a lot of talk at the Greek restaurant about this, Marie said). Politics was unstable. Inflation in the UK would soon be running at 30 per cent.

•

K's newly acquired second-hand Roneo duplicator was coming into its own. He kept it confined within the labyrinth that was Des's workshop. It was a medium-sized machine of grey metal which stood on its own grey metal cabinet wherein one could store reams of paper and supplies. He had learned which stationery stores were best to buy the supplies cheaply – mimeograph stencils and canisters of ink – and how to inject the ink into the cylinder until it was at the right level (too much and the ink flooded everything, saturating the stencil wrapped round it and thence the paper that passed through the rollers; too little and the stencilled texts were barely even transferred to the paper). You could print in a colour other than black – blue, green and red inks were available, for instance – but that necessitated either cleaning out the cylinder thoroughly between colour changes or (more practicably) investing in spare cylinders for each colour. K's duplicator was an electric model, so could be switched on and the thing could be left to roll automatically until the stack of paper in the input tray was exhausted. But there was a risk inherent in this, for inevitably there'd be a mishap at some point, usually a paper feed glitch, necessitating an emergency shut-down; so it was safer on the whole to crank the thing by hand, especially if only a small edition of maybe less than a hundred copies was being planned, which was normally the case. Once done, each stencil could be carefully unpeeled from the cylinder, and then hung up with clothes pegs on a line with the others to dry, whereafter they could be re-used if needed for a second edition. The smell of the ink and of the stencils was extremely pleasant. Gestetner stencils were incompatible with Roneo, and vice versa, in a precursor of the Apple/IBM personal computer wars that were still a good ten or fifteen years in the future. The stencils were prepared by the simple method of inserting them into the typewriter instead of paper and typing onto them. If an error was made, and a wrong character was typed, you had to apply a tiny blob of pink error-correcting fluid, which looked and smelt like nail varnish, to the offending character or characters, wait till that dried, then reverse the typewriter carriage to the exact position, and retype over the obliterated mistake.

One of the treasures Des had found in his daily trawls of skips and abandoned offices was a heavy manual typewriter with an extra long carriage. This unwieldy machine was a godsend; for it enabled K to feed the pristine stencils into it in landscape rather than portrait orientation. Thus was enabled a primitive method of imposition: you could type facing A5 pages so that they could be printed side by side onto the space of an A4 sheet. With careful page planning, an entire A5 booklet could be printed, which, the pages once collated, could then be centre stapled (using a long-arm stapler): a sophisticated variant on the standard A4 side-stapled publication.

This was the format K chose for his first self-published poetry collection. He bought a ream of grey duplicator paper for it – yes, cool sophistication was the intended effect, though in the end it would actually look a bit tatty. And Des was now into silkscreen printing, and promised to silkscreen a moiré pattern for the cover on some rather natty A4 sheets of card he had found in another skip, which were a rich and lustrous red on one side. And so a hundred copies were printed, collated and bound, which was a great achievement, though in truth even a few weeks later K began to feel secretly the final effect was not quite as good as it had been in his imagination, and even more secretly that some of the poems – he had selected what he thought were his best so far – were beginning to be a bit embarrassing. Nevertheless – he took them to Compendium Bookshop and the friendly man behind the poetry counter immediately purchased six copies at 35 per cent discount, giving him the cash from the till and placing the booklets then and there on display on the shelves of the vast small press poetry section, which was amazing. There was also Bernard Stone's Turret Bookshop in Kensington, dedicated entirely to poetry, a shambling little store with poetry crammed at every angle in every nook, up to the ceiling, and an unnerving, life-size waxwork of Sigmund Freud, for some reason, standing in suit and waistcoat in one of the aisles (looking startlingly like John W, K thought). Bernard Stone himself was a man of few words: he would inspect the merchandise offered him; then he too took six copies for sale of everything that was verifiably poetry.

And in this booklet K also now had possession of an exchange token in the internal economy of the small press poetry world. He gave Mike a copy, and Mike returned with a copy of one of his own things, and he met Paul who ran the Enterprise readings in Camden Town and gave him a copy too, and Paul reciprocated with copies of various publications of his own press, and promised him and his cohorts on the magazine, *Alembic*, a special reading in the upcoming weeks, and also told him if he was planning more poetry publications he should send him a copy of everything he did. Paul told him it was essential also to go to the Dada and Surrealist evenings organised by Bernard Kelly, the mad Irish Dadaist, who was very strict about whom he allowed to read, that is, whether they were deemed sufficiently Dada or Surreal, but there was one coming up the following week in a pub in the Fulham Road, where you were allowed in free if you were carrying an umbrella. K did not possess such an item, but thought he might try it.

Mike said he was thinking of leaving London, and invited K to stay with him in his cottage near Hebden Bridge, Yorkshire, where they could plan future literary activities. He had rented the cottage for next to nothing; it was near where Ulli was then living, Ulli who was then called McCarthy but later changed his surname to Freer, who had long blond hair and looked like a frazzled rock musician, and whose poetry was just crazy and beautiful. In truth, K could make little of it, but in conversation with his friends Robert and Peter later he had likened it to action painting, with a dazzling array of words and verbal gestures just flung onto the page, apparently at random but maybe with an underlying purpose that was not fully understood even by the poet himself, and Peter much later had said that allusion had been useful and a key to what was going on.

The weekend K got round to visiting Mike in the cottage he found it was in essence a wreck – no heating, panes of glass missing in the windows, an outside toilet, a long way from anywhere – and also Ulli was not in residence that weekend, so the plan to get together with him did not come off. Also living in Hebden Bridge at the time, mentioned K, was the other Paul, the one who did *Curtains* magazine, with the French connections, full of theory and advanced pornographic art, Paul Buck, that was it, but Mike didn't know him. Anyway he and Mike had some good chats over the weekend, consuming a few bottles of red wine and smoking a few joints in the process, and agreeing that Mike would publish K's next work, a set of prose poems, and he would publish Mike's, in an A5 landscape format with a cover to be silkscreened by Des. Also, they decided they would collaborate on a theatre production at the Oval Theatre (he had contacts) based on a character in one of K's short stories, the one that had been published in that prestigious Anglo-American literary journal – which greatly excited Mike. At least, that was the impression K had that they had decided before it all got too much and he eventually zonked out in his sleeping bag in Mike's attic.

•

The stereo in the communal living room was mostly commandeered by Des, who played such albums as *Dark Side of the Moon* by Pink Floyd and *Tales From Topographic Oceans* by Yes incessantly. Music that was dense and rich, with a timbre that was always on the verge of being hysterical though in other ways too controlled, too weighty, still carrying a memory of the insubstantial shadows of creation from nothingness but already starting to succumb to the law of entropy. Punk had yet to explode – a year or two from now, but nobody knew this of course. Whether that would make a difference, well. Anyway, at this time K more and more was wanting to play free jazz but he felt he had to confine it to the record player in his room, because of the "What's *that*?" reaction from various people at various times. Though he found that June rather liked Cecil Taylor, she thought he was far out.

His eyrie at the top of the house with its commanding view over the rooftops of London, was also a refuge from social interaction. When it all got too much. For the doorbell rang incessantly. Often – sometimes several times a day – it was Big Steve. Large and dishevelled, unshaven, with a skin condition and straggly black hair, fag hanging at the side of his mouth, his great powerful hands hanging at his sides, there he was again on the front doorstep: Is Des in? he would inevitably ask. Des would give him jobs to do for small amounts of cash in hand – helping with removals or heavy lifting – and in gratitude Steve would scrounge items from skips or dustbins that he thought Des or other members of the household might like and bring them round hopefully, like a cat depositing the gift of a decapitated mouse on the doormat. As often, he would simply arrive in hope there was a joint on the go so he could get stoned for free, or else that there was something to watch on the colour TV in the communal living room, or even better, that he could get stoned *and* watch some TV – for the word had got round the neighbourhood that the Sunderland Terrace household possessed a colour set, and many of the local Patchwork residents, hippies and street people were eager to avail themselves of this resource. In truth, Big Steve, unlike many, was genuinely good-hearted. Unlike many, that's saying something indeed though not enough. For instance, the one or two certifiable almighty cunts in the neighbourhood. Big Steve, he was all right. But not the brightest of buttons, perhaps. There was a story that he had been temporarily employed on the Patchwork workforce and told to dismantle and take out an unusual and possibly valuable wrought-iron spiral staircase in one of the houses Patchwork was renovating, and, not understanding the brief, had simply smashed it into a heap of twisted metal. But maybe that was just a story, spread by people who wanted to discredit him for some reason. Steve lodged in another Patchwork house, in Durham Terrace just down the road, which, compared to the Sunderland Terrace regime, was chaotic to an alarming degree; the household consisting of a long-haired *paterfamilias*, called Dave or Danny or Denny, it varied depending on who you talked to, maybe in his thirties or forties, rumoured to be a heroin addict, who ruled the roost with his adoring female companion/wife ever in tow, a long-dressed and voluptuous hippie chick who was suckling their first-born child; but in addition two other very young Scottish girls who wore patchwork clothes and smelt of patchouli whom he was reputed also to be fucking, although some said snidely the Scottish girls were only interested in each other; and completing the ménage a pack of dogs of various sizes that roamed free – the attic of the house, bare-boarded and unfurnished, being given over entirely as a den to these animals, who decorated its floorboards with piles of faeces that went uncleared. It was, then, this household that Big Steve, who also owned a dog called Tank that followed him morosely sometimes, was earnestly trying to escape from, and if the truth be known he was dying to be asked to join the Sunderland Terrace community, but even kind-hearted Des baulked at that.

•

Down in the basement, which was sealed off from the rest of the house – the communicating door being locked and bolted – a separate thing was happening; there was a different regime entirely. It was Sean's domain, and he lorded over whichever elements of the Irish freak scene happened to be around. Eileen rented a room down there, and Patrick, who was sweet on her, visited frequently. But there was a lot of coming and going.

Sean came upstairs (via the front door) to say that Eileen was cooking a meal and everyone was welcome. It was a vegetarian Irish stew, if such a thing were possible. But only K and Phina were in. Marie was working, Meryl was in hospital, Keith visiting her, and Des and June were away at a festival.

K and Phina went down to the basement, first exiting at the front door of the house, descending the steps from the street and being re-admitted to the building. The lighting was dim, the scent underlying that of Eileen's cooking a mingle of damp and of burnt wood and ashes. It was a matter of common knowledge that the incumbent prior to Sean, a Jamaican named George, had attempted to set fire to the building in his own DIY version of the Gunpowder Plot. But he was long gone; now there had been a regime change. And a very large joint was being passed around, and so the stagnant air acquired a new and pungent aroma. In addition to those named, there were two or three others, mainly seated on the floor, vaguely familiar from Patchwork general meetings or day-to-day interactions, forming a subterranean constellation of long-hairs. The dog Dennis, Sean's dearest companion, a terrier-ish mutt, visited each of the guests in turn in the wake of the monster reefer, his nose no doubt picking up valuable information. It was a peaceful scene, though Patrick was holding forth quite vigorously.

The main theme of Patrick's discourse was that Patchwork, for whom he and one or two of the others present worked as a general builder, was not so much part of the "alternative society" but in essence an imperialist organisation founded by idealistic English public schoolboys, dependent upon a labour force comprising mainly the Irish working class. This analysis elicited several knowing nods and sympathetic laughs.

The dope was powerful, which enhanced the deliciousness of Eileen's stew when the dishes were eventually passed around, while also adding to the general hilarity. Dwarfish Sean presided over the proceedings, squatting in a corner, nodding and grinning. Dennis the Magic Dog, having vetted all the guests one by one, tail wagging, settled down finally next to him. General talk happened profusely. Everyone chipped in. They talked about the Birmingham pub bombings, the implications thereof for all in here and at large. The talk then turned to first experiences of living in London and the UK. Neither K nor Phina could remember whether it was Sean or Patrick who memorably described arriving at Paddington

Station for the first time, back in the day, and seeing the long line of taxis. Sure I blessed meself, he said, I thought it was a funeral.

And of course, then, beneath the hilarity that ensued at that point, a funereal quality was also created, a miasma that hung. Or maybe it didn't. Maybe it didn't at the time, and it was only retrospective, activated much later within the protocols of memory – and whose memory would that have been? In the weeks and months and years that followed, K certainly retained a memory of little, sweet Phina laughing uproariously in her corner, maybe at that remark, which probably had been made by Patrick, or at something else Sean said, though Sean was not that much of a wisecracker, but he had definitely taken a shine to Phina and had directed many of his interventions in her direction – that K did notice – at the time or thereafter. But K thought subsequently of that evening among the subterranean Irish crew with apprehension, even something close to gloom or despondency. Not that he ever mentioned anything about it. So: hindsight. At any rate, he and Phina said their goodbyes at the end of the evening and, stoned and slightly weary, exited by way of the steps up to street level, Sean holding back the still eager Dennis, who wanted to accompany them; then re-entered the building at the front door, said goodnight to each other and retired each to their bed, in K's case to await with pleasure the arrival of Marie from her restaurant job in the wee hours of the morning which were not so far away now.

•

Blue continuous glow of the paraffin heater's pilot light in the middle of the bedroom. The paraffin would run out so quickly. A fat fly taking up residence in the warm room, heedless of the incense wafting. Whisky from a Chinese cup sitting on the low wooden bedside table. The fabric of everyday life – almost a thing in itself, a thing you could smell. A poem written under the influence of Peggy's grass. Books by other poets arriving through the letterbox. Tim Buckley died. A letter in the post from Bernard the Dadaist, including a photocopy of a crazy poem detailing the activities of police walkie-talkie crooners. He was organising a poetry event in anticipation of the coming referendum on continuing membership of the European Economic Community, to which he was vehemently opposed. The arrival of the last quarter of the twentieth century, and everyone seemingly in a gross stupor, a mass of neurosis, hardly able to stand. From downstairs, the faint sound of Des in his workshop singing falsetto. A consultation of the I Ching revealing nothing of worth. Footsteps, who could that be.... The *Cabinet of Dr Caligari* on late-night TV. It is necessary to destroy appearances sometimes to reveal the infrastructure (but if there is no infrastructure?). Fifty pages in and still nothing is resolved, nothing revealed, the labyrinth merely extending itself a little more, the centre, whether holding or not, no longer being visible. The bowels make strange noises – is this the echo of the Big Bang? Flash of a kestrel, unmistakeable, visible in the London sky through the bedroom window. Watching the football on TV, Big Steve has crashed out in the next room, very stoned, complaining he "can't get up". The communal living room was cleared for a meeting of Patchwork Housing Association, and subsequently for a jumble sale, which took £27 in receipts. People constantly ringing up, wanting to leave messages for the people next door, for Sean or the other people in the basement, for Big Steve, for people in *next door's* basement, one of them being a very fat woman named Pat Dolan for whom there was a particularly urgent message (seems she was getting married) and on knocking to convey this the door was answered suspiciously by Johnny, the Asian transvestite, wearing a short white nightie revealing thin, knobbly knees. About a dozen assorted people staying for the weekend, including Charlie, a spastic. (Yes, that was how they referred to the condition then.) They drank copious coffee, ate potato omelettes.

K in orange T-shirt, combat jacket, jeans and tennis shoes wheeling the bicycle through the park, and afterwards riding it through the deep streets to sign on at the SS, cold hands slipping on the gears, traffic bearing down, in touch with the gods, including those of primordial devouring and ingestion. Dangerous customers. But the magic images wheeled round him, and he could not be touched. The sun came out. And so on to Bishop's supermarket in Porchester Road round the corner from Westbourne Grove, where at the delicatessen counter scraps of various cold meats were sold off cheaply at the end of the day.

In Barclay's Bank on Westbourne Grove one day, where he stood in the queue to cash his giro, he overheard a conversation between two other customers:

How are you?

Would be OK, if it wasn't for those damn squatters.

Oh yes?

They're all up Sunderland Terrace and Durham Terrace, the police say they can't do anything. It's a disgrace blah blah, what's happening, it's the council who's to blame, blah blah blah.

Yeah I blame the council. But surely something can be done about it?

We don't get a say, do we, blah?

And so on and so on.

•

K was still planning with Mike to make progress on this play they were talking about putting on at Oval House, but in the meantime he'd written a suite of semi-disconnected poems and dramatic monologues developed from the second of the stories he'd submitted to and had been subsequently published by the prestigious Anglo-American literary journal, of which more later. And that involved roping in friends as participants – Robert and Peter to read the texts, sometimes simultaneously, and Keith to play guitar, because K's own guitar skills were as yet rudimentary, and Keith was a pretty good twelve-string player though on this occasion he produced the Japanese Les Paul copy he had recently acquired and did an excellent job on it, though the amp fed back and the speakers packed up – while K himself took the title role, a Bowie-esque doomed rock star, Brylcreeming his hair and wearing his sister's boyfriend's blue sequinned jacket and somebody else's lurex shirt, and the poetry audience loved it, first at the University of London Union (Robert's friends in the London University Drama Society had secured this gig) and then at the Enterprise in Camden Town. The show, like the short story on which it was based, was called "Jasper Dean's Final Statement" with the maybe-pretentious strapline "a sound collage of poetry, rock and increasing entropy". Almost the entire Share household turned up to the first performance. Mike did the first half of the show, along with Dada Bernard, who opened with a "potato poem" which involved attempting to blow up a potato with a bicycle pump, unsuccessfully, for the bit on the end of the pump promptly flew in the air and hit K on the nose as he was sitting in the front row. Afterwards, with the equipment loaded in the van, Des drove to Dulwich where a friend of a friend was having a party with some good sounds – Hendrix, Little Feat, Bowie – and people danced with their faces painted. On the way home at 2.30 in the morning, an impromptu theatre event was being enacted in front of the brand new Kentucky Fried Chicken place on Westbourne Grove, a West Indian in a huge tam and an unusually tall Scotsman larking around with a tiny tramp. It was kind of balletic.

K was on a roll at this point.

Then there was Liverpool, another actually paid reading at Atticus Bookshop (thirty quid plus travel expenses as per Poets' Conference/National Poetry Secretariat rates); subsequently ferrying 'cross the Mersey, entering the futuristic space of the Metropolitan Cathedral, tipping the third-place horse in the National, visiting the bleak, boarded-up space where the Cavern once was, staying overnight with Robert, getting pissed on Guinness. K read the poems he had written at Dover and some more since, which were going to be in the third of his pamphlets to hit the streets (the second, a prose poem sequence, having been published by Mike's imprint as an impressively austere black-on-white production), with his own Surrealist collage on the front using an image of Erik Satie, the best thing he'd done yet, for which he'd received a subsequently treasured postcard from no less than Jeff Nuttall, who had scrawled "Lovely stuff!" And at the Enterprise he promised to publish a pamphlet by the series curator, Paul Brown, this time perhaps with an offset-litho cover he could get printed on the machine at the Hampstead Centre.

The Little Press Bookfair at the National Poetry Centre in Earl's Court, organised by the Association of Little Presses, whose driver was the irresistable force that was Bob Cobbing, provided an opportunity to sell poetry pamphlets and magazines – and K's personal experience was that nine items were sold for a total of £1.70, all of which was subsequently spent on other people's publications, as was the custom, so that these were in effect zero-sum transactions. To the Hot Pot then for a meal with the poets, lots of animated talk, all about who was interesting and who wasn't; analysis was brief and uninformative, but the poets knew what they valued and what they didn't, and if you knew you didn't need to speak and if you spoke you probably didn't know. It was just like that. Nobody talked about good or bad, it was "interesting" or "not interesting", and almost by definition the vast bulk of contemporary poetry, especially contemporary poetry in Britain, was consigned to the "not interesting" category. And then returning to hear readings by Chris Torrance, Colin Simms, James Simmonds, who were all deemed really interesting, and they were. And so back to Sunderland Terrace for *Match of the Day* followed by a late-night horror film on TV, enhanced by more dope-smoking. Both the spastics, Richard and Charlie, were enthusiastically present. Marie at work the while it seemed; finally crept into K's bed at 7.30 in the morning, where the fuck had she been?

•

"Yoooo ssssilly sspaaaastic!" That was Richard, upbraiding Charlie for something allegedly dumb he had done. Right from the outset it was part of their banter, and Charlie giggled.

The fact that two young men with cerebral palsy, affecting them to different degrees, were casually referred to as "the spastics" is hard to understand forty years later. But also that they bandied the term among themselves in ironic fashion, like two young African-American dudes calling each other nigger. There would have been a line beyond which you could not venture, but where was it?

Richard had come first. June introduced him to the rest of the household one long, cool spring evening. A large man in his early twenties with curly hair and sleepy blue eyes, who walked with a shambling gait and stretched his words out forever. He said a regular feature of his life was being picked up by the police on the street late at night and trying to convince them he was not drunk and disorderly, that that really was the way he walked and the way he talked. He could look after himself pretty well, most of the time, though it might be said electing to have muesli for breakfast each morning (he pronounced it "mmmoooooooz-uh-lee" with great relish) was not the best decision, as there was inevitably many a slip between the bowl and the lip, the spoon shuddering uncontrollably in his grasp, and much of the milk and cereal ending up covering a wide target zone centred roughly on his place at the table. But he was an amiable fellow, everybody agreed. Marie got on especially well with him.

June's vision was becoming reality. She was well ahead of the times. The vision was this: that there was no reason why people with disabilities should not have the opportunity to live as they wished, outside of institutions, and that included embracing alternative lifestyles such as shared communal houses. (She was later to come under fire from others in her profession when it was discovered that, shock, horror, young spastics were being allowed, unsupervised, to live in settings where drugs were freely available, and no doubt sex was too.)

Charlie followed. Charlie's disability was more severe than Richard's. Thin and wiry, with glasses and long lank hair, he ambulated solely with the help of a walking frame, could climb and descend stairs by hanging onto the banisters but then required someone to carry the walking frame up and down after him. He needed help at mealtimes but could go to the toilet on his own. Outside the house was a different matter: he drove one of the three-wheeler one-person vehicles that were licensed at the time; it was startling to see his powder-blue car careering down the street and round corners, but he was in complete control. Never more so. He did embrace life, it did not harden or on the whole disappoint him, and he was tough. Others who visited the house incessantly saw him in different ways, often kindly and with understanding, sometimes without, speaking deliberately and slowly as though to an idiot which he was emphatically not, but you have to expect that unfortunately.

Charlie had an A1 poster of Blondie's Debbie Harry tacked

up on the wall of his room, the pink slash of the mouth, the white shock of the hair. He was a big Manchester United fan. Now it turned out Manchester United were visiting Loftus Road on Saturday, almost in the neighbourhood, to play Queen's Park Rangers, who were then riding high in the First Division, and K and Charlie discussed the possibility of going to the match. Charlie would need help getting into the ground, therefore needed to be accompanied, therefore could not drive there, as his car was strictly a one-person vehicle. But then, although for an able-bodied person it was a reasonable walk to Loftus Road, it was too much for him and his walking frame. The solution was for K to wheel him in the wheelchair and be his official minder. Will we be able to get in, K wanted to know, and Charlie, experienced in these things, assured him they would.

Match day, the usual throngs, the usual stalls selling footballing merchandise in the streets, the powerful scent of hot dogs. In those days you could just turn up even to top matches, queue briefly, pay your money at the gate and you were in. But coming up to the turnstiles, K was once again assailed by doubt. No way would the wheelchair be able to go through that narrow entrance. Yooooo wwwwwait, said Charlie, nodding confidently. And then, magically, without anything having to be said, a yellow-jacketed steward appeared, beckoned, opened the big gate next to the turnstile and ushered the two of them through. Neither of them were charged or asked for a ticket. Inside the gate, steps up to the terracing. No problem. More stewards appeared, and lifted the wheelchair with Charlie in it up to where the bright green of the pitch suddenly came into view and the powerful hubbub of the crowd exploded into their ears. They showed Charlie and K to a clear space where they had a good view of the end of the pitch. They were good-humoured and made jokes.

"I tttto-o-oldyoooo ssso!" exclaimed Charlie, beaming.

Unfortunately, his beloved Man U lost 1-0, a David Webb

header sealing the victory, and it would have been worse had Stan Bowles not missed a penalty. But it was a good day out for Charlie, and K enjoyed it too.

•

But it was all up, down in the basement. There was a rumour that Eileen had fled – sacked from her admin job in the Patchwork office and even threatened with the police because she allegedly had been embezzling the accounts. Allegedly. Everybody tight-lipped about that. Sean looking grim. Also he told Des that Dennis the Magic Dog was no more. Dead. Run over. No further details.

A full moon. Pressure gonna drop. Another in a series of Patchwork emergency meetings in the Sunderland Terrace living room, about finance and the future. Things were not looking good generally.

Saturday. Sean came upstairs to watch *Match of the Day* on the communal TV – cause for apprehension, as he was already drunk and clutching a large bottle of cider, but he behaved, more or less. Before leaving, he begged K to make him a cheese sandwich, as he was skint, he said, and hadn't eaten all day; which K reluctantly did as Sean staggered around the yellow-painted kitchen, muttering. He ate it swiftly, and disappeared downstairs.

Sunday morning, a commotion. Phina was weeping, wouldn't say what the matter was. Her cheeks wet, and with what looked like a bruise. Her friend Meryl was summoned from her room. The story came out in fits and starts. Late Saturday evening she'd answered the door to Sean, who told her that's it, he was off, going back to Ireland next week. The heat was on him, he'd said. He was getting rid of most of his possessions, and wanted her to have a look at some bits and pieces she might like to have. She had been quite touched by this. So she went down to the basement with him, nobody else around. He'd been friendly and full of chat, but she'd smelt his breath, he was very drunk. Then he started getting over-friendly, ended up demanding she sleep with him, she refused, he struck her across the face, then dragged her to bed, kept her there all night, raped her. He threatened her with a knife – said he would keep her locked in the room until he left for Ireland, taking her with him. All this she told Meryl, wouldn't talk to anyone else. Somehow she'd escaped upstairs, perhaps when he was asleep, it was unclear.

Everyone in the household was devastated. Someone mentioned going to the police, but nobody else took any notice. Phina refused anyway. Somebody else mentioned "sorting Sean out". Nobody volunteered. There was no sign of Sean now.

Meryl had taken charge anyway. She said she was going up north for a week to see her parents, and Phina agreed to go with her.

•

Three and a half months went by.

Two o'clock in the morning. Des heard K was up, or saw the light was on, for he was writing, and came into his room. Sean's back, he said.

Oh, no.

He was drunk again, and being very heavy. He'd been with Des in his workshop all evening. Des had finally got rid of him, and come upstairs with half a joint for a little smoke before going to bed. We shouldn't let him into the house, said K. We said we wouldn't. Why did you?

You can still hear him from the basement up here, said Des, avoiding the subject. He opened the window, and sure enough the unmistakeable sound of Sean shouting incoherently wafted all the way up.

Another week went by.

It was Midsummer's Day. K was alone in the house, making himself a cup of coffee in the first-floor kitchen. Sounds of footsteps coming up the stairs.

Sean. How did you get in?

Door was unlocked.

Sean had a pint bottle of heavy stuff in his stubby hand. His pale eyes were bleary. He said, You've got to help me, K. I need help.

What kind of help?

I'm an alcoholic, he said. I'm in bad trouble.

K tried to ignore him, moved into the living room. It was hot. The French windows onto the little wrought-iron balcony were open, letting in a bit of a breeze. Sean followed him, holding onto his bottle. He started the conversation again.

You're lucky to have this house.

How's that, Sean?

It's my house. Patchwork gave it to me. Ask Greg Moore. Ask Henning. Ask Bruce. Greg Moore gave it to me personally.

Oh, yeah?

Yeah. You know, I'm trying to hold it together. I threw Colin out of the basement, because he was dealing bad stuff and not paying the rent.

K wasn't sure who Colin was, but he knew Patchwork had said Sean had paid no rent for the past ten weeks.

Come on, K, let's have a contest of strength, suddenly said Sean, setting aside his emptied bottle and putting his huge pink elbow on the table.

K refused.

See, that's why I don't like you. That's why I don't like you. Because you're not a man.

Being a man isn't just a question of physical strength.

Don't fuckin' lecture me. I'm giving you fair warning. Don't fuckin' talk to me like that. Because I'll fuckin' push you over that balcony.

Sean glared mistily and tottered.

K's stomach knotted.

Sean turned round and stumbled out of the door, making for the stairs. K stood stock-still, eyes closed.

If he were a man, K supposed, he should have pushed Sean down the stairs for his parting shot, which was

Tell Phina I fucked her.

Then he was gone. K heard the front door bang a few moments later. K was overcome with feelings of hatred, and also of self-hatred, for not reacting, for being weak and pusillanimous, for failing to take charge of the situation, but how, but what should he have done, but but.

Some time later the front door opened again, but it was only Des.

What's been happening, it's wet all down the stairs, phew. For fuck's sake, someone's peed on the stairs, said Des.

Door was unlocked said K, who was still trembling.

Sean?

Yeah.

•

By the end of the summer, Sean had disappeared again. This time he never returned. Nobody ever saw him again. One of the Patchwork people reported he was banged up in Pentonville prison, not for the first time. For assaulting a police officer.

•

Before all this had happened, before the first winter had set in, and then that hot summer that followed, with Charlie and Richard arriving, and before K's employment at the Hampstead Centre and his subsequent happy meeting there with Marie, and Marie moving in, and all that ensued thereon ... before that, there was the incident of Bode's breakdown, afterwards known as "the freak-out", which needs to be related.

But this was the prelude:

A short story by K had been accepted for a prestigious Anglo-American literary journal. He had been ecstatic about that. It was a breakthrough. And then the story was actually published. It was called "Second Coming", an ironic allusion to the Yeats poem. It was the best thing he had done yet: a mini-portrait of the end of the world, mysterious, poetic, with dark humour, compact and yet resonating. There it was, in print, in a proper perfect-bound volume, not a side-stapled A4 mimeographed production, alongside internationally recognised names, and he received a cheque in the post for fifteen pounds and two copies of the magazine to show people. One of the people he showed it to was Bode, who was impressed, and congratulated him.

And the magazine had indicated it was up for further submissions, so K sent another of his recent stories, and was promised publication of that too, in a subsequent issue.

A few weeks later K noticed a job advert in *Time Out* posted by this same prestigious magazine, looking for an editorial assistant for two days a week. About now, K had started to get hassle from the SS. A part-time job of this sort would get him off benefit and still leave him plenty of time to write. So he applied, and the same editor who had accepted his story invited him round for an interview.

The journal's address was a smart house in a residential tree-lined square in South Kensington. K arrived, chained his bike to the railings, mounted the steps and knocked on the big shiny black door. It was opened by the editor himself, a quietly-spoken but affable American gentleman, perhaps in his late fifties, who ushered him into a book-furnished living room with a huge bay window overlooking the square, and offered him a cup of tea.

They chatted about writing. The editor asked K about his literary influences, and K mumbled some things upon which he later reflected and felt embarrassed by. The editor explained that the journal appeared quarterly, but he had other, additional plans. He was going to branch out into book publishing. He could use some help immediately. He offered K the job there and then, starting next Thursday. Sorry, the pay would be quite modest, but. Would that be all right?

K was in heaven.

The following Thursday morning he turned up again, and the editor greeted him warmly, showing him into the same comfortably appointed living room. They were not alone: the editor introduced him to two or three other young men who were sitting around a table talking and drinking tea and coffee. He accepted a coffee. The conversation was quite desultory, but K got the impression that these guys were all employed by the journal in some capacity. After some polite exchanges, K felt obliged to take the initiative. What would you like me to do? he asked the editor.

The editor frowned, and considered for some moments. Then he led K into the back part of this open-plan upper ground floor and showed him some shelving in an alcove. On the shelves were past issues of the magazine, going back several years, randomly stacked; also piles of other copies here and there on the floor. You could start by tidying up all this, the editor told him vaguely. Could you file all the back issues in date order on the shelves?

K said that he could.

The editor apologised that it wasn't very interesting work, but he hadn't properly sorted out what there was to be done yet. K said there was no problem, and, getting to his knees and setting his coffee mug on the carpet beside him, went to work.

While he worked diligently at sorting the magazines and restacking them, from left to right, starting at the upper left shelf with the earliest issues he could find – which went back a couple of decades – he could hear the rumour of conversation that continued between the editor and the other young men. One appeared to have retired to a desk and was doing some work himself, probably proofreading or copy-editing, but the others continued to converse around the table. He couldn't quite hear the content of the conversation. Once, he looked up, and noticed one of the young men passing over a newspaper to his companion, who looked intently at an article for some minutes. He saw that the title of the newspaper was *Gay News*. This gave him new pause for thought.

By midday, he had finished his task. The editor thanked him. There was no more work to be done for the day, he told him, but tomorrow he would start in earnest. The editor apologised for not being better organised.

Back at the house, he found Bode had let himself in. He had returned from Bristol and was planning to stay till the end of the weekend, before going on to Dover. K was glad of the company, because Des and June were away at the Edinburgh Festival, Meryl was currently in hospital and both Keith and Phina were separately visiting parents in Yorkshire, so the house would otherwise have been empty.

But Bode was in a strange mood. He said he had been wandering around London. He had walked from Waterloo Station, across Westminster Bridge and into Westminster Abbey, where he said he had knelt beside the bust of William Blake and meditated there for a while. He said London was "crumbling under the strain of time", its buildings all askew. At the shrine to Blake he had felt he was in "resurrectional time", and in the deep stillness there he had found the answer: to see England as the jewelled crown, the New Jerusalem, in a world centred on the true idiom of the Lord Jesus Christ.

K talked with Bode for an hour or so about Blake. He sensed that for all Bode's talk of being at peace he wasn't. But he could not understand what was really going on within Bode's mind.

Towards evening, K said he proposed cooking a meal and offered to share it with Bode. But Bode said he wasn't hungry, and retired to his room to read.

•

Now this was how it happened: the stillness of the night was interrupted by an almighty crash of breaking glass, a ghastly human howl, then more crashing and pounding. Terrified, K glanced at his illuminated alarm clock. It was two-thirty in the morning.

He opened his bedroom door. Bode, stark naked, was running up and down the stairs incoherently. When he saw K in the doorway, he scuttled up to him, fell to his knees and clasped him around the waist, as though he were the Saviour. Bode's body was white, rubbery, sweaty, and he was babbling. Then, to his added horror, K saw that blood was streaming from his right wrist.

What the fuck is going on? cried K, but there was no sensible answer from Bode, only ravings about Jesus Christ, Rudolf Steiner, time, space, Einstein, blind springs, blood, water, the "I" (or possibly "the eye"). But he spoke in a way that assumed he was being understood and empathised with.

There were drops of blood all the way up and down the stairs.

Bode, you've hurt your wrist, said K, let's go in the bathroom to sort it out. But Bode escaped his grasp, fled back into his bedroom, where K found him smearing his blood over the cover of his Bible, as though this would staunch the flow.

Finally, K succeeded in persuading naked Bode, blubbery, wild-eyed, still dripping blood, into the bathroom. He made him step into the bath and hold his wrist steady under the shower. Yes, sir! yes, sir! shouted Bode in response to every command, now parodying the role of a servant being ordered about by a white master. Diluted blood washed down his arm and disappeared down the plughole. Bode started giggling. Then he became very concerned. The blood continued to well. Have I cut an artery? he asked, suddenly sober. I don't think so, said K as the water continued to flow, just hold still. I've cut an artery, said Bode, I'm sure I have, I need to go to the hospital!

K remembered there was an accident and emergency department within a half-hour walk. Just get dressed, he said, and Bode, mocking his authoritarian manner the while – Yessir! yessir! – nevertheless obeyed his order.

As they walked along the pavements at 3am, nobody about save the odd fleeting cat, Bode, his hand and wrist wrapped in an improvised bandage, calmed down and became almost rational. He said there had been extreme bad energy flowing through the house, and he had had to break windows to let it out. He was astonished when K said he had felt no such thing. For it had been palpable. Anyway, he had used whatever came to hand: his alarm clock had been the first object to be hurled through his bedroom window, followed by several books – "including *Life Against Death* by Norman O Brown" he specified. (He reminded K that they must look for that one in the garden in the morning, as it was important to him.) After this he had gone into the living room and thrust his fist through a pane of glass in the window there, which is what had caused the injury. He explained that the reason for this was to create a channel for the bad energy to flow out.

The A&E department at the hospital was quiet, and Bode was seen to quickly, by an affable Indian doctor. Ah, you have been a naughty boy, then! he exclaimed jovially. We will ask no questions! Bode smirked, and winked sidelong at K, who sat there impassively. Have I cut the artery? inquired Bode politely, as the doctor cleaned, stitched and dressed his wound. No, no, of course not, said the doctor, this is very minor, I assure you.

Bode and K walked back to the house. I'll be OK, I'll be OK, said Bode, in response to K's anxious queries. They each retired to their own room.

In the morning, K knocked on Bode's door and asked if he wanted coffee. Bode emerged, tired-eyed.

Over coffee, K asked what Bode had been frightened of. He replied that as he lay in bed it seemed to him the bed was actually a slab of marble, and he sank into it. Becoming part of it, he had entered into a realm of what he called deepest timelessness.

So it was like a near-death experience? inquired K.

Bode assented. He seemed almost normal. But then he added: And yet I myself was still in time and so able to swim a whole line of people to the island that I'd reclaimed from the river of God's intelligence during the second fall.

What the hell did this mean?

I need to go to work, said K. It's the second day of my new job. At that magazine that took my story, you remember?

I have to get to Dover, said Bode, to my wife and kids. Can you take me to the train station first?

K said he didn't have time.

You see, I'm the marginal man, added Bode, by way of further explanation. I'm going in and out all the time.

K advised Bode not to travel; he was not in a fit state. But Bode insisted he would be better off with his family. This was indisputably true. K didn't know what to do. There was nobody else around; no-one would return to the house before the weekend, there was nobody he could ring and talk to. Even his parents were away on holiday in Spain. His sister was in London, but she would have gone to work by now, and there was nothing she could realistically be expected to do to help.

OK, said K reluctantly, I'll actually take you to Dover.

That would be fantastic, said Bode.

K rang up the magazine office and spoke to the editor. He explained that a close friend had suddenly been taken very sick and he had to stay with him. He was extremely sorry; it was not good practice, he admitted, to default on the second day in a new job, but he would make it up, he would come in an extra day the following week. The editor said he understood, and wished him well.

K and Bode travelled by tube to Charing Cross station, where they bought tickets to Dover: one return for K, one single for Bode. Bode had some money to pay for them.

Bode said little on the journey. He mentioned that during his perambulations around London the day before he had felt himself in dialogue with intelligences "vastly superior to ours", who had been guiding him. Through such intelligences he had learned the inner significance of the letters of the alphabet, and how the English language in particular had been formed to give complete expression, in moving, loving terms, to the cry-of-I that was Christ. He added that this had been a humbling experience.

By the time the train reached Dover, though, he seemed back in his senses, speculating on what the weather was going to do for the rest of that day, saying he was looking forward to being back with his family. Alighting on the platform seemed an immense relief to K; it was breezy and sunny that afternoon, it was like a different world, it felt like coming out of a fetid tunnel.

But at the train station exit, Bode suddenly turned, shook K's hand and said goodbye. K was startled; he assumed he had been going to accompany Bode all the way home and leave him in the hands of his wife. No, no, you've done enough for me, insisted Bode, please go back to London, I'll be all right from here on. And he turned away again, his rucksack on his shoulders, and departed without another word.

The house was still empty when K got back. He went to bed and slept for about twelve hours, exhausted. In the early morning, the phone rang: it was Bode's wife. She sounded very worried. Bode had not actually arrived home until late in the evening; she gathered he had spent a few hours wandering around the Dover clifftops before heading home. She thanked K for his care, and said she would report back on what was happening.

Later that morning, the phone rang again. It was the magazine editor. He was very apologetic, but he said he had made a mistake. It seemed there was not after all sufficient work to justify a job for K. He thanked him for his trouble and said he would post him a cheque to cover two days' labour.

•

Two days later, Des (who had repaired the broken windows on his return from Edinburgh) drove June and K to Dover in the van to stay for a couple of days with Bode's family and provide what support they could for his wife, whose name was Elsa. They actually lived in a farmhouse some way out of Dover, near the cliffs.

Elsa was Scandinavian and serene and the children were beautiful, a boy and a girl, five and seven years old, both ash-blond like their mother. Their paintings were tacked on the walls around the house. The other inhabitant of the house was an elusive orange cat named Pushkin.

They all went to visit Bode in the psychiatric hospital near Canterbury, where he had agreed to be committed for a short time.

Elsa was worried because she had to be on shift duty as a

midwife for the next few days and without Bode had no-one to take the children to and from school. That, it emerged, was why Bode had been making for Dover this weekend before the cataclysm. There being no-one else available, Des and June having other claims on their time, K volunteered to do this.

But first he had to sign on at the SS again, so after the hospital visit he returned to London in the van with Des and June to do so; then hitch-hiked straight back to Dover. A Spanish lorry-driver set him down in Dover town centre.

He had trouble finding the house again, getting off the bus from the town centre at the wrong place and having to walk through miles of countryside before reaching his destination. A moon-faced barn owl, ghostly white, appeared on a post in a field as he approached.

Then disappeared.

When he'd been here with June and Des days earlier a sleeping bag had been found for him, but now he had a nice bed in the spare room. For the next three days, K and the two children bicycled to school each morning while Elsa was at work. The children chatted about the go-kart they were constructing in the shed. Cows, spiky with straw, blinked at them from their ragged pasture.

The idea was that when Elsa had finished her shift she would fetch them home in the afternoon. And that worked quite well.

K walked along the clifftops. He looked at the lighthouse through the telescope he had borrowed. He looked over the edge of the cliff at the gulls circling below, and the grey, hissing sea, and thought of *King Lear*.

The fields above were quite flat, and a mist was coming in, smudging the trees and the distant grain silos. At the edge were clumps of sea-spinach, wild cabbage and a few rabbits rutting in rough lesions in the chalky earth. A breath of wind cauterising the nerve-ends. Poetry was in the air, a kind of throat logic.

Breath burning skin, radio waves.

Cleft of a greybacked egg.

Back in the house, K cleared away the kids' breakfast things. Then he sat down at the rather beautiful upright piano in the living room and idled his hands over the keys. He had no idea how to play the piano, didn't even know where middle C was, but he made up chords, Cecil Taylor style. Once, while he was doing this, Elsa came into the room and smiled. She said: That sounds good. I really have no idea what I'm doing, protested K. You have a nice touch, though, she said. He didn't believe her. He couldn't repeat it, what he had done, what he did.

Sometimes he sat at the table and did some writing. He didn't have the Olivetti with him, but he had his notebook.

The sun finally broke through the clouds and in through the window, obscuring the picture on the television set. There were six oranges in a bowl on the sideboard and on the coffee table a mound of pine-cones and apples in another bowl. On the mantelpiece were little collections of stones. The piano chair had a bright patchwork leather cushion on it. There were books and Russian Orthodox ikons everywhere, and, to his surprise, a poem of his that he had typed out and given to Bode some time ago was tacked on a wall.

K had been dreading the visit to the hospital with Des, June, Elsa and the ash-blond kids. But it had passed off all right. Bode had been discovered, looking quite well, sitting in a chair in his dressing-gown in a sky-blue-painted ward with orange curtains through which the sun beamed. He showed them a bright abstract picture he had produced on a small piece of board. They're teaching me to be a painter, he said sheepishly, a glint in his eye. A pause. It was all in the timing with him. Actually, it's shit. Then they all laughed, with relief perhaps. He sat back, put the artwork down. Behind him was a large, empty birdcage.

It wasn't the end of the story.

•

Another autumn now arrived. Rain dribbled down the window. An old friend of Phina's, Rob, joined the household. The lifetime of the house was uncertain; nobody knew how long they had before it would be coming up officially for renovation, to be repossessed by the council, but when wasn't there uncertainty? There were now weekly meetings, and a rota for cooking and washing-up, but there was resentment bubbling under. Three cats wandered in and out: Fortnum, his sister Mason, and tiny Houdini, found scared in the street and adopted by Marie. Other people came and went. There was another wave of bombings attributed to the IRA, said the radio. At 1.30 in the morning the rotten floorboard at the foot of the bath gave way. The temperature dropped and the nights drew in.

Charlie dislocated his elbow. He had gone in for a 10-mile charity trike ride, had come off and hit the track badly on the thirty-third lap. For most people, this would be an inconvenience. For him, it had a domino-fall of consequences. He was now more than ever dependent on the others in the household: had to be put to bed at night and got up in the morning, washed, given his bottle to pee in, a whole panoply of other things. That lasted about a month. He couldn't wait to be free of it.

There were quarrels between K and Marie, followed by remorseful making-up sessions. No two days were similar, yet life went on regardless. Buying muesli from the freak shop in Portobello Road. Santana played the Hammersmith Odeon; several house members went to the gig, and June made some special dope cake for the occasion. Another Christmas came and went. Sunshine, chocolate, incense and dope. There was a party in the house: Charlie more or less back on his feet now, jigging on his walker, Richard staggering into everyone's way. After midnight, Marie and Rob sitting on the floor in K's room playing cards while K read on the bed – Weather Report's "Unknown Soldier" on the record-player. Stoned and floating. The ghost sound of Bode typing on his portable typewriter in the next room. Charlie taken by K and Rob to see Queen's Park Rangers beat Leeds. Howard Hughes was dead. Compendium Bookshop took twelve copies of the latest issue of the poetry magazine K edited with Robert, freshly collated and stapled, and sold out within a few weeks. Greater London Arts had agreed a grant of fifty pounds to fund the next two issues. Big Steve had taken up with a girl called Esther, and he brought her round; she acted strangely, seemed to be going quietly round the bend. More IRA bombs. The house opposite had been devastated by fire during the night; in the morning, nothing remained of its roof but charred guts, and later in the day uniformed men were observed scrambling around nailing down polythene sheeting. It was all floating.

Winging it

This is a room on the 19th floor of the St Regis Sheraton in New York City. It is approximately the size of a badminton court. One end is occupied by a king-size bed, plumped up crisply and whitely, with a quilted backrest. There are bedside tables on both sides, on one of which is a white telephone. To the left of the bed, as one sits on it, is a huge TV set and in front, in the middle of the room, a grey velour sofa supplied with multi-coloured cushions; also a glass-topped table on which rests a crisp, folded, complimentary copy of the *Wall Street Journal*. Near the TV is a small refrigerator stocked with beers, miniatures and Coca Cola in traditional bottles. To the right of the bed, against the striped wallpaper, is an inlaid mahogany desk with a green desk lamp and a potted plant. Bentwood upholstered chairs are placed at various positions in the room. A chandelier hangs from the ceiling. At the far end of the room – though the wall is mirrored, giving the impression of even more space beyond – is the door to the dazzling ensuite bathroom, where the toilet seat has been secured by a paper tape bearing an official guarantee of hygiene.

The heavy curtains in the bedroom are sombre in colour, and they frame large windows through which are visible other high-rise buildings. The sounds of the city below are scarcely audible: taxi horns, the occasional police siren. In the rectangles of space visible between the buildings, misty clouds drift.

This for the next two or three weeks is K's domain.

•

The taxi he hired at JFK took him to the wrong hotel at first. It wasn't the taxi driver's fault; the Rock Star's London office had neglected to mention that the hotel had been switched at the last minute. By the time he discovered what had happened, via a number of telephone conversations in the lobby, the taxi had long departed, and he had to engage a new one to take him and his suitcase from Gramercy Park to the right hotel, a few blocks distant. The replacement taxi driver was more talkative than the first had been. He said his mother had just passed away at the age of 89 in Russia. Three years ago he had gone to Russia to see her for the first time in 40 years. He then went on to describe his immediately previous client: an enormously fat guy who had eaten peanuts continuously throughout the ride. That guy's just sick, he said. It's quite a common thing in this country, these people, you know, they're love-starved, so they just eat until they get repulsive, he said. That was his opinion. And it was a free country, he was entitled to express it, thanks to the First Amendment.

Weird feeling. That was jet-lag, he supposed, it didn't kick in immediately. He was shown into this palatial room. Didn't know what to do next. Late evening by now. What would it be in London? Actually, he felt a bit wired. Tired but wired. He went out, pulled the bedroom door shut behind him, went down the corridor to the lift, sorry, elevator, and out into the dull heat and clangour of Fifth Avenue. Traversing the blocks, getting the hang of it, he discovered a small cinema tucked away on one of the parallel streets. The film it was showing was *How the West Was Won*. He paid the few dollars and went in to watch the movie. Apparently it was showing continuously, you could walk in at any point. It was immensely long, in fact it felt like a lifetime, and some way through the process, he was not sure at what point in the film, because he couldn't remember whether it had actually finished and started again or not, at some point without noticing it he began falling asleep, and thereafter the golden scenes of the movie flowed into each other like a dream. He didn't understand any of it, but it passed.

The tour had been postponed for a month because the guitarist, Wee Jimmy, broke his hand. Things had happened for K in the interval between first meeting the Rock Star at his home with the Rolls Royce, the Paolozzi, the jukebox and everything, and now – not all of them good. For example, it was all over between him and Marie. Things had deteriorated. They hardly saw each other after she'd elected to work extra hours at the restaurant, and they bickered when they did meet. And also, Bode, as part of the recuperation following his second breakdown – which will shortly be described – gave up his intermittently occupied room and departed the household for good on a spiritual trip to India, and so Marie decided she should move back out of K's room into the newly vacated space.

Meanwhile K had got to meet his prospective tutee, the Rock Star's daughter, Buttercup, for the first time. The meeting took place at her school, under the watchful eye of the head teacher. Buttercup turned out to be a young-looking thirteen-year-old with long fair hair and a puzzled expression.

She chewed on a red lollipop throughout the meeting, wanting to talk mainly about her passion for horses. The head teacher confirmed privately that she was very behind in English and maths particularly, and gave him some textbooks to use. The following day, experiencing a curious feeling of spatial and temporal disjunction, K paid a visit to the Rock Star's office in central London. The Rock Star was not present. Plush, brash, cool, wide rooms. The Head of Administration, a trim, handsome lady in her early forties with short dark hair and blue eyes, needed to talk to him about his visa, his flight and the arrangements for him to be paid. The Rock Star had not wanted him to be on the same *per diem* expenses as the rest of the tour party, she revealed, but she assured him confidentially that this would be arranged, and that he would also be on a retainer of £25 a week for the unexpected month before departure.

The day before departure the sky was overcast and it was cold. Harold Wilson had resigned and James Callaghan, beating off Michael Foot's challenge, had been elected Labour leader and therefore became Prime Minister.

Walking along a London street under the grey sky, K came upon a large modernist glass and ferro-concrete office building, its vertical acreage being of the deepest and most luminous blue. Then he realised the building was in fact reflecting exactly that portion of clear blue sky that was hidden from him by the other buildings. The feeling he got from that was something akin to grief.

Things were not great in the household generally.

Marie had promised see him off at Heathrow. But she didn't show up.

•

There is a knock on the door as K, definitely jet-lagged, wrapping himself in a substantial white bathrobe with the St Regis monogram displayed on the left breast, emerges from his shower. It's the man in charge of financial admin and expenses for the tour. He is the first member of the tour party K has met since arriving. He is in a dark suit with a white open-collar shirt, but a little dishevelled, as though he has slept in it. Lank hair, pink complexion, cheerful.

He has brought with him the promised room list: a location guide for everybody in the tour party, comprising some two dozen individuals, including tour manager, admin and PR staff, roadies and members of the band, tour photographer, tour artist-in-attendance, all their names listed by room number, excluding the Rock Star himself and his family, who are booked into a different hotel which has to be kept secret, possibly even from the band. The tour manager and the band members are shown as having "suites", the others "rooms". But this document, printed on expensive-looking laid paper, is just one of a collection, also including pages of instructions and helpful information about the hotels and locations in the itinerary over the next two and a bit months, all housed in a black faux-leather ring binder branded with the band name and tour logo embossed in gold, and on this particular personalised copy K's own name in gold-embossed Gill Sans caps in the lower right corner. The St Regis will be the default hotel for the East Coast phase of the tour, explains Financial Admin Man, and the band members and the roadies will be flown or bussed out each day for gigs from the New York base: Detroit, Philadelphia, Boston, and so on. As for K's duties: he is to remain at the hotel each morning awaiting a phone call from the tour manager or from the Head of Administration, to let him know whether he is required to teach Buttercup her lesson that day. If he is, arrangements will be made. If not, he is free for the rest of that day.

Financial Admin Man hands over a hundred and forty dollars cash in various denominations. That's K's *per diem* expenses for the week, twenty bucks a day. He is advised to keep all receipts for travel and subsistence, and to present them weekly to Financial Admin Man. On hotel restaurant and room-service bills, he should sign at the bottom (making sure to indicate his room number) and write the words "add 20%". That is what is expected as a tip here.

You ready to teach young Buttercup? says Financial Admin Man as he departs. K affirms that that is his role.

Well, good luck, then, sniffs Financial Admin Man. He adds, as an afterthought before closing the door behind him: The previous one didn't last long.

•

Shortly after Financial Admin Man has gone, the white telephone purrs, with that American single tone so familiar from the movies. K picks it up. It's the Head of Administration. She wants to know how he is. Also, she needs to tell him the name of the hotel where the Rock Star and his family are staying, under the assumed name of Mr & Mrs O'Sullivan: it's the Stanhope, on Fifth Avenue, facing Central Park. This is strictly confidential information, given to K on a need-to-know basis, and not to be imparted to anyone, not even other members of the tour party.

K feels very important.

He will probably be called on Monday morning to give Buttercup her first lesson there, but he is free for the rest of today, Friday, and the weekend.

Um, says K, I have a question.

Shoot, says the Head of Administration, in her posh English voice.

The Financial Admin Man just told me Buttercup's previous tutor didn't last long, which worries me a bit. Can you tell me any more about that?

There is a brief silence.

He wasn't really suited to the role, says the Head of Administration. He just wasn't right for it. He was on the Australian tour last year. He ... departed midway through. It was by mutual consent.

Mutual consent.

That's right. Don't worry, you'll be fine.

Thank you.

K realises now he is hungry. Emboldened, he picks up the phone again and dials room service. He orders breakfast. Twenty minutes later, there's a knock on the door, and here it is: served by a suave waiter in a white monogrammed jacket (the same monogram that is on K's bathrobe), on a trolley-table, covered by a thick, deep-red tablecloth, that moves smoothly and utterly without sound on its castors. Freshly squeezed orange juice, egg and bacon under a silver cover, toast, coffee in a silver pot. He signs the bill – add 20%. The waiter smiles discreetly and withdraws.

•

First Marie had moved out of K's room (after the arguments, principally about her freedom to come and go as she pleased, had crescendoed into hot rows, ebbed into remorse, repose and kisses, flared up again and finally petered out into sullen silence); then she had declared her intention to move out of the house altogether. The Greeks had offered her the possibility of a bedsit above the restaurant, which obviously would be a great deal more convenient for the job.

But before that, Keith and Meryl were on the way out, returning north to Yorkshire, where they were to get married, and in their place had come Rob, an affable guy with twinkly eyes and a goatee beard, an old college friend of Phina's. He could talk football with Charlie and K and so got on particularly well with them. He later installed his girlfriend, Sylvia, in his room, though she was very shy of the rest of the household and kept aloof. Phina herself was on her way out too, intending to live with her sister when they could get a place together.

Bode had come back, and occupied a vacant room. Temporarily, it was said. He was off the medication, he said. When Elsa and the kids had sorted things out, they were all going to live in Ireland. That was the long-term plan. Actually, for a short while, amazingly, Bode became the mainstay of the household. He was back to being lucid, and when he was lucid he was organised. He insisted on weekly house meetings and proper rotas for duties such as cooking and cleaning. He mediated between Des, whose unconscious tendency was towards totally benevolent autocracy, and those other members of the household who were pissed off by this. He became the guardian of Process.

It was a while before all started to go wrong again. Bode's disappearances resumed. Then a phone call from Michael, his South African friend in Oxford who was training to be ordained into the Russian Orthodox priesthood: had we seen Bode recently? Only, he had been staying in Oxford with Michael and other friends, but had left his bike and his backpack and vanished. He was on the loose again.

And next day, a day of weird sultry grey weather with fitful wind only slightly relieving the dense warmth, Bode did turn up at Sunderland Terrace on his bike. His behaviour was odd, erratic – mysterious smiles, gnomic remarks that didn't seem to make much sense – and K feared a repeat of the incident of the previous year, all the props and circumstances being the same, including Des's and June's temporary absence at a festival. He stayed a day or two, then suddenly, as evening approached, put on his backpack and crash-helmet and departed. Those who were around retrieved bizarre typewritten notes on small scraps of paper that had been strewn around the house. None of those made any sense either. Also fragments of a torn pound note and charred leaves of blank paper in various locations. Phina said she had come downstairs to the kitchen, sleepless, from her room at six in the morning to find him smiling and holding a cup of tea in each hand, offering her one – as though he'd known in advance she'd be down. Meryl, on her last day before leaving the household with Keith, reported she'd encountered him on the balcony of the living room – the one Sean had threatened to throw K over – with his crash-helmet on, jigging and dancing to music that was playing softly on the stereo.

Oppressive grey weather continued. June's friend Maryla, who was staying with the household temporarily while thinking about moving in permanently, reported that money was missing from her room. That was not good. Phina was disgusted to find a deposit of shit in the fireplace of her room. Had one of the dogs from Durham Terrace got in?

At the Hampstead Centre, where K was doing a day's work, he mentioned these worrying events to John W. He related everything he knew. What should they do about Bode? He was scared Bode was having another psychotic episode and there was going to be another almighty show-down. The current members of the household hadn't experienced that.

John W frowned and stroked his beard. He said: Can you repeat that?

About Bode?

No, you said you found shit in someone's room?

Yes, said K, apparently a dog must have got in.

You do know that defecating in inappropriate places is a not uncommon behaviour with people having psychotic episodes?

K did not want to think about that.

He's frightening people. I don't know what he'll do next, said K.

John W said if his mental state became unmanageable and he seemed a danger to himself or others the thing to do was to phone the duty social worker. They would assess the situation. Commitment under the Mental Health Act was then an option.

When he returned home, there was an animated discussion taking place. Rob, Marie, Maryla, Phina, Charlie. Richard was not around. Des and June were still away at that festival. Bode was flitting in and out. He had locked himself in the bathroom and run a bath. He had been heard shouting and chanting in there. When people had knocked on the door – the bath water was seeping out from under it onto the landing – he had not responded. Nobody knew what to do. When he finally emerged, clad only in a towel, it had been impossible to engage in a sensible conversation with him. He had explained he was literally holding the house together, holding the ceiling in place, and the walls. He had reported that space and time were turning inside out.

Where was he now? Up in his room. Someone thought they had heard the clatter of his typewriter.

We have to get some help, said K.

At that point Bode came down. He was fully dressed, looked quite normal. Hello, he said.

We think you should leave, Bode, said K. Go back to Dover. Go back to your family.

Bode stared at him with the semblance of a smile.

What is more important, he asked, the point or the eye of the needle?

You're frightening us, said someone else.

I'm sorry about that, said Bode. The answer is: the eye to the needle is love, the point to the needle is love, and the thread that we pass through the eye of the needle is love. It's the gold thread that connects the I Am to the I Am.

Everybody agreed that love was the answer.

Will you go back to Elsa and your children? said K.

Bode did not reply, but went back up to his room.

K found the number of the council social work department in the Yellow Pages, and rang it. He explained the situation, and they said it did sound like an emergency and someone would be round shortly.

You shouldn't have asked him to go, remonstrated Maryla. They were all sitting around the dining table.

Was that Bode clattering down the stairs? Was that the front door closing?

The Honda 90, normally chained to the railings outside, was gone.

The doorbell rang. It was the duty social worker, a pleasant, middle-aged man in a tweed jacket and jeans. He came upstairs. They all sat round talking to him. Someone made tea.

So he's no longer here? How has he been?

Bode's recent doings were narrated.

And before that, how was he?

K said: He's had these episodes before. I've seen one, last year. But then he seemed to calm down. He's been quite rational for months. Actually, I thought he'd been really down recently, didn't seem very happy. But then suddenly he becomes the opposite, completely manic. Do you think he's manic depressive?

Sounds more like schizophrenia to me, said the social worker. But there's not much I can do if he's not here. Please ring me back if he returns.

Bode did not. But someone reported having seen him on the Honda, cruising round the neighbouring streets.

He had left the bath in a mess. There were traces of shit melting into the plughole, what looked like used tampaxes, nuts and bolts and small plastic objects, possibly collected from around the neighbourhood, scattered in and around the bathtub. Clearing up was not pleasant.

K went to work again at the Hampstead Centre the following day. On his return that evening, he found the front door open. Des was in his overalls, at work replacing the glass in the door panel, which had been shattered.

Bode?

Yeah, Bode, said Des shortly.

How was the festival?

Good.

So where's Bode now?

Gone. He's taken all his belongings this time. Think he's gone to Michael's place in Oxford. Michael said he would ring us. Elsa's been in touch.

There was peace for a week.

Charlie was probably on his way out. He had recovered very well from his dislocated elbow, and he was quite cheerful, but there was opposition from outside to his living in the communal house. Some of his family apparently were not very happy. Nobody in the house wanted him to go.

Richard wasn't feeling well. When he'd had a drink, his speech distorted even more than usually. I'm uh fffeeeeling reeeeeee-uh-ly shshshitty! he declared to anyone who would listen after a couple of pints in the pub down the road, the Durham Arms; the articulation hanging in almost endless suspension. He was feeling the pressure, attributing it to "London", and so took himself off to his mum in Bristol, his doctor having told him to take a month off work. But when he returned he seemed no better, the charged atmosphere in the house following the latest Bode episode having got to him: he began to yell and have temper tantrums about what seemed nothing in particular. Occasional inexplicable behaviour too, but lacking the imagination of Bode's weird fantasies. Des thought he too was having a psychotic breakdown, but K was of the opinion he was just very depressed at having no girlfriend and feeling unloved. One evening he disappeared, and then two cops arrived on the doorstep with him in the middle of the night: they had found him wandering in Chelsea, lurching about. They were quite gentle with him. He was barefoot, and bewildered.

June and Des were summoned to Greg Moore's presence, there having been discussions about the Sunderland Terrace licence coming to an end, and the possibility of a permanent shared house in Kingston upon Thames, part of Patchwork's phase two development. But when they arrived in his room, where they discovered him drying himself in front of the fire after a bath – in preparation, he said, for a City of Westminster cocktail party – he appeared to have forgotten what he wanted to see them about. Anyway, yes, it would only be a matter of months before they would have to move out of Sunderland Terrace; so when K finished his US tour with the Rock Star there might well be no home for him to return to.

•

BB is the tour manager. A larger than average man in early middle age tending to corpulence, with short hair, serious-faced. K is summoned to his room at 11.30am, where he finds him wrapped in the regulation St Regis Sheraton white bathrobe, sitting at his trolley-table having his breakfast. He indicates an easy chair, and K is seated. K had thought his own room palatial; this is colossal, actually a suite, with another room visible through an open connecting door. BB speaks at some length about his concern for Buttercup's welfare and general education. He wants K to know he has his support if there are any problems. Any problems at all. He says Buttercup's education programme will start tomorrow, Monday. Is today a rest day? Not at all: there have already been two dates in Detroit, and today the band and roadies are being flown to Toronto for tonight's gig there. But he, BB, will personally take K over to the Stanhope on Monday morning for Buttercup's first lesson.

In reply to a polite query, K says he finds the hotel depressing. BB nods sympathetically. The clientele seems to consist chiefly of middle-aged and elderly couples, the women, curiously, often looking older than the men. There seems to be a huge turnover of sheets, towels, tablecloths, but not much joy.

Back in his room, K feels guilty. He should have been preparing lessons, but instead he rolls, lights and smokes a joint. From outside the window comes the distant and intermittent sound of someone playing the saxophone, rather indifferently. Or is that cars honking now? He turns the TV on and uncomprehendingly watches a live broadcast of a baseball game. He's intended to catch a Carolee Schneemann film and lecture down in the Village, but he's missed it. He switches to the PBS channel, which seems to show nothing but British TV programmes, mainly BBC. Sitting on the bed, he resumes his reading of *Gravity's Rainbow*. Strewn all over the bed are multiple sections of the *New York Times*, several pounds' weight of them.

•

Monday. Nothing happens for the entirety of the morning. At 12.30pm the phone finally rings. It's BB, very apologetic. The family, he says – "the Family", we know who we mean – have decided actually to take the kids to tonight's gig in Ohio – and the plane departs very shortly. So K's services will not after all be required. He is to stand by tomorrow, but he's free to do as he pleases today.

He decides to walk downtown and catch a cinema showing of the recently released *All the President's Men*, with Robert Redford and Dustin Hoffman re-enacting part of the spectacle that is the ever ongoing collapse of the American Dream. Meanwhile, on the TV news the candidates for the next Presidency continue to re-enact their own spectacles.

•

Tuesday. Nothing. Nothing and nothing. No sign of BB. K tries ringing his room, and then the Head of Administration's. No reply. Leaves messages. Frustration. Continuing to read *Gravity's Rainbow*. Walter Cronkite on the news: a lorry loaded with ammonia plunges off an overpass onto the freeway below; an ex-mental patient goes berserk with a gun and kills three people; doctors report that liquid marijuana drops may be a cure for certain types of blindness, but patients "would have to put up with side-effects of euphoria". At 7pm it starts raining heavily outside. The phone goes. It's the Head of Administration. More apologies from her. Lessons with Buttercup will definitely begin tomorrow.

•

Wednesday. It has been a warm, close night. Strange nightmares of being chased. K wakes to real sirens in the street. BB calls. K is to meet him downstairs in the lobby this morning.

With BB in the hotel lobby are the Rock Star's housekeeper, a familiar face from that first meeting in the London house, and also a huge, amiable guy called Jeff, a former American football player with enormous horny hands and a moustachioed grin. He is the bodyguard. They all get into a limousine that has pulled up outside, and are whisked off, through Central Park, arriving very shortly opposite the Metropolitan Museum, where they get out and cross to the Stanhope.

The Rock Star's family have rented a suite in the hotel, which is more or less a self-contained flat. They are ushered through. There are sounds of children laughing in the other room. The Rock Star's wife appears, her blonde hair in a ponytail: Hi! she greets BB, and shakes hands with K when introduced. We met before, she says. The kids are playing, she adds, Huey's little girl is over this morning.

Huey is the tenor sax player in the band, K remembers. Or maybe the trombonist? BB starts talking seriously to Mrs Rock Star about tour business.

While BB is thus engaged, the Rock Star himself comes through the door, in an open-necked white shirt and jeans, grinning broadly. He greets K like an old friend; motions him to a sofa.

Hi, K, it's really great to see you, he says when they are both seated.

Nice to be here, returns K cagily, and how's the tour going?

Great, we've already had some good gigs. Really good. Now, you're here to teach Buttercup?

Well, I hope so. Looking forward to it.

You know, it was her head teacher said she needed a tutor on tour. As far as I'm concerned, well, Buttercup's learning quite a lot on the road, you know?

Well, I'm told she's a bit behind on some of her school subjects....

Yeah, the head said so. A bit behind. A child her age, she should know her times tables and that. Well, the head, she got together with your friend, John W, and so ... I guess, here you are!

Here I am. I'll try to do my best.

And I appreciate that, K, I really appreciate it, you know. The thing is ... Buttercup's doing really great, she enjoys being on tour with us. The kids are having a wonderful time, they really dug the gig on Monday night. Buttercup is learning so well. She loves it. Now I need to tell you something. The thing is ... it's hard, but we really care about family life. I do. The whole thing is, we're trying to be just an ordinary family, you know, an ordinary working class family.

In really extraordinary circumstances? ventures K.

You're right, really extraordinary. That's absolutely right. But we try hard not to let it get to us. We just ... we live as a family.

I do take a professional pride in my work, said K. I won't let you down. Just as long as certain conditions can be met. That is, (he blustered), as regards regularity of daily lessons and all that. I was told you needed Buttercup to have a daily lesson. That's fine with me. But of course, if you do need to cancel a lesson for any reason, well, just let me know in advance....

Of course, of course. No problem. You can trust us. And we need to trust you, right? Well, I know we can trust you.

You certainly can.

Good man. Good man. Oh ... BB?

(BB is trying to attract his attention.)

Are we off? Sorry, K, gotta go. Violet will take you in to see Buttercup. I think we've got a desk set up somewhere, where you can work. OK?

He offers his hand as they both rise from the sofa. Philadelphia here we come, he cries jovially, in a comic approximation of an American accent. And within a few moments he and BB have gone, and Violet the housekeeper is there smiling at K. Buttercup is ready for you now, she says.

•

Three more days have passed, and K has now taught Buttercup two lessons. The first was pretty trying. Buttercup was sullen; clearly and absolutely did not want to do schoolwork when there was a rock'n'roll tour to enjoy. Not to mention being distracted by her little siblings and their little friend who were in and out of the room playing and giggling, chased by the ever patient Violet. The second lesson, two days later, was much better: she had started to come out of her shell, actually went to work willingly on the tasks K set her; she had even begun to smile now and again. Still, she's a proper little madam, Violet mentioned to him in an undertone when they were out of earshot of everybody.

The only downer was that K had a mild ticking-off at the start of the second day's teaching. The thing was: now he knew where the Stanhope Hotel was located, and realising it was only a few blocks from the St Regis, he decided it was ridiculous to wait to be picked up by limousine, so instead he made his own way there on foot. Which took a matter of less than fifteen minutes. Only, when he arrived at the Stanhope, went up to the reception desk and asked for the suite where the Rock Family were installed, he met a stone wall. The desk clerk denied any knowledge of the hotel's illustrious occupants. But then quite by chance K did locate them: the Rock Star himself was spotted talking with BB and some other people in the tea-room, with one of the security staff – not Jeff – standing guard outside. So he managed to attract their attention, and someone instructed the desk clerk that he had been vetted and it was OK to let him go upstairs, and all was well.

But later in the day he had a phone call from BB. He was not to take his own initiative in this way again. When summoned to give Buttercup her lesson, the procedure to follow was to ring Violet, who would ring the limousine service, and wait in the lobby of the St Regis for the car to arrive. The driver would deposit him at the other hotel after a drive of a few minutes. He was to tell the desk clerk he had an appointment with Mr and Mrs O'Sullivan. The management would ensure the reception desk had a note of the appointment.

Now it's the weekend again: no lessons for Buttercup. K wakes every morning feeling guilty because he has not used up enough towels. Every day the chambermaids deluge him with mountains of fresh white towels; also hotel-monogrammed books of matches pile up, regardless of how many have been used (and they are only used for the occasional clandestine joint). A mint chocolate in silver paper is deposited on his pillow when the bed is made up, starchily and tightly, each morning. The chambermaids smile, but speak hardly any English. Make bed, sir? They move silently and deliberately from here to there and back in their soft slippers. K tries to remember what the rules are about tipping them. He spends a lot of time watching American TV. Live baseball seems to be on around the clock; he is beginning to get the hang of the rules. Exceptionally, there is a live soccer match: the New York Cosmos, with an ageing Pelé in the side, along with former Spurs reserve Mike Dillon. He listens to his portable cassette player: Herbie Hancock, Miles Davis. While he is doing this, he watches the Miss USA pageant with the sound off. It's hot, and the weather's muggy outside. There has been a parade down Fifth Avenue this afternoon. The Miss USA show seems to go on for an eternity. Now Miss Minnesota is being led out, with a single red rose in her hand. Is she the winner? But she's not weeping, just smiling dazzling white, so maybe not, and then a few more get the red rose treatment, so perhaps this is a short-list. The short-list, that's what it is. A discreet knock on the door: it's the club sandwich and coffee he has ordered from room service. Add 20%. That reminds him, he's had a bill of 57 dollars from the hotel for extras; he will need to chase Financial Admin Man for the second tranche of his weekly-paid *per diem* expenses so he can settle it. Now the results. And yes, it is indeed Miss Minnesota who has won, and the tears start to flow, as he imagined they must.

•

K's first encounter with the teenyboppers. Leaving the St Regis in the limousine with Violet and Jeff, he notices a small gathering of very young women, children really, some with cameras clutched in their hands or dangling on their necks, gathered in small groups close to the entrance. And then, which is more significant, on arrival at the Stanhope there are more young people, again mainly girls in groups of two and three, waiting around in the street outside with hope in their eyes. One girl has actually got into the hotel lobby – looks nervous, eyeing K and Violet silently as they wait for the elevator. So the Stanhope has been rumbled; despite all the elaborate security precautions, the fans have taken no more than a week to breach the defences.

The lesson today is cut short, as Violet is due to take the children to a movie. She offers to get K dropped off at the St Regis on the way, so out they all go, downstairs and through the lobby, Violet, Buttercup and K, with the two little ones. The girl fans are still hanging around; they part to let them through; but as the two adults and three children wait for a taxi in a tingle of light rain at the kerb, a few come forward, producing cameras, some of them quite elaborate and expensive-looking SLRs, and begin snapping the little group nonstop. You don't mind, do you? asks one. Violet ignores them. Another calls out to Buttercup: How's it going, Buttercup? Buttercup, clearly used to this, smiles wanly under the silk of her long fair hair, but says nothing. One of her younger siblings hides behind Violet, the other grins shyly. The yellow cab pulls up, but the driver won't take more than four, so K says not to worry about him, he'll walk back to the St Regis. As the cab pulls away, some of the teenies continue to snap their cameras after it. Another small group make to follow K as he starts his walk, then quickly decide he's not interesting, and melt away. But a group of three or four continue to cluster patiently around the hotel entrance under a grey sky.

•

Curiously leaden still, that sky, and leaden too K's movements, his limbs sticky and warm, which is due partly to the weather but also – but mostly – is a consequence of social activities unconnected with the Tour Over America, social activities in which drink and drugs have played a part. For his tutor services aren't required, he is told, during a period of a few days when the tour party, including the family, are away in Atlanta; and he is free to do as he pleases.

He's made contact by phone with Rhoda, a girl he met when Des brought her back to the Share household last year, where she stayed a few days during her London visit. (He had encountered her in the street during one of his excursions, found she had nowhere to stay and had taken pity on her.)

Now Rhoda apparently lives only a few blocks from where K has found himself – well, a few streets laterally and quite a few blocks uptown – and she recognises his voice on the phone even before he's said his name, even though she never received the letter he sent her before leaving London.

She says she just lost her job and has been living on unemployment, but she's about to move in with some friends of her new boyfriend, Richard. Because Richard values his independence too much, doesn't actually want to live with her, not yet, she confides. But does he (K) want to join them at Richard's apartment for a meal the following evening?

So he takes the Broadway bus uptown, because the distance is longer than he estimated, finds the apartment, which he thinks wonderful. Richard, a good-looking man in perhaps his early thirties, is a percussionist, specialising in contemporary classical repertoire: in the main living room is a huge gong in a frame ("tam-tam" Richard corrects him), no fewer than two vibraphones, or perhaps the other one is a marimba, K cannot remember the difference, and a baby grand piano, and there is still room for a dining table which is laid for five. The other human guests are a couple who have travelled from downtown Manhattan, but the other beings in the room are four lean, angular, menacing cats which stalk the spaces silently; two of them, Rhoda, explains, are hers, having been evacuated from the apartment she is now abandoning; and the current experiment is to see whether all four can live together, even though Rhoda herself will not be joining them. They seem to be accomplishing this so far, mainly by staying out of each other's way. So the wine and beer flows, the food is delicious, topped off by a magical pecan pie that is Rhoda's speciality, which K finds doubly delightful perhaps because by then a couple of joints have been produced and passed around, tiny ones rolled with powerful grass, not the massive carrots favoured in the UK, and, well, by then *everything* is delightful. The conversation does tend to centre on him, for he is an object of interest because of his current gig, and the other four are agog to hear what life is like on the road with the fabled British Rock Star; but towards the end of the evening it veers towards other topics, at first baseball, because there is a big game on and Richard switches on the TV to catch some of it, and it turns out the other man in the room, Richard's friend and guest, whose name is James, and who is there with his wife Lee, in the course of clarifying some of the finer points of the game for K's benefit reveals that he too is a poet and – miracle! – interested in the very same kinds of poetry as K is, and moreover is embarking on editing a magazine, the imminent first issue of which will include John Ashbery, Ted Berrigan, Diane Wakoski, Allen Ginsberg, Ed

Sanders, Anne Waldman, names that are legendary to K – therefore there is an exchange of phone numbers before the evening is out, so that James and K can continue the conversation.

To his amazement, it turns out to be nearly one in the morning. How will he get back to his hotel? Use the subway, of course, he is told. Yes, they do run all night – doesn't he know?

Over the following day, the lassitude slowly leaves K's body, and he even manages to nip out in the afternoon to a Third Avenue cinema to catch the earlier Martin Scorsese movie *Mean Streets*, which was recommended by one of the gathering at Richard's apartment during a discussion of the recent hit *Taxi Driver*, and excellent it is; and then his recurrent depression is lifted temporarily again when his telephone buzzes and reception tells him he has a guest, James Sherry. So James enters the room, where he and K spend an hour chatting busily about poetry against the background hum of the air-conditioning, and K gives him a spare copy of the magazine he co-edits, *Alembic*, and asks him to submit some of his own work for the next issue, which he will be organising with Robert back in London when the tour is over. They find that K is already familiar with the work of many of the US poets James is planning to publish, though not all of them – James particularly recommends he get in touch with two Manhattan-based poets who are friends of his, Charles Bernstein and Bruce Andrews, who are also planning a magazine – whereas on the other hand James is not at all familiar with most of the British names K mentions, but promises to start looking them up. James invites him to a forthcoming poetry reading in the East Village, but it's on the eve of the tour's departure for the next stage in Chicago, so K says regretfully he may not make it. But anyway a transatlantic accord has been established.

•

He meets the Head of Administration to touch base over a burger and a milk shake, at a joint round the corner from the St Regis. She wants to know how he's getting on with The Daughter. Not great, he admits. The Daughter's school skills are indeed rudimentary, and she is not very motivated to improve them. He has suggested that, wouldn't it be a good idea, as her English homework, to keep a diary of the tour – but all he's managed to drag from her is a few banal and ill-spelled sentences. ("Violet took us to the zoo. We saw some animals.") The Head of Administration says she's not having a great time on this tour either. She reveals she has been working with BB for four years and with the Rock Star for three, but has recently started to wonder whether it's time to move on. I mean it's fantastic in some ways, she says – you know, I'm sure I saw Fred Astaire in the hotel the other day – but –

As she pays the check for them both, she asks him whether he would like to attend the New York concert. Yes, he would. Perhaps she can arrange that.

•

It is 2am in the dimly-lit bar of the St Regis Sheraton, where a dreary pianist in a tuxedo croons softly over caressed ivories for the benefit of a sparse and mostly elderly audience that do not appear to be paying him much heed.

Dee, the rhythm guitarist, occasional bass player and MD of the Rock Star's band, is relaxing, drinking and chatting animatedly with Huey, the sax player. They are joined at their table by K and Financial Admin Man, who were earlier discussing expenses. Financial Admin Man has handed K a big bunch of dollar bills representing the next tranche of *per diem*, and also some extra for travel, which is separate. He snorted with derision when K presented him with evidence in the form of bus tickets. Bus! You took the bus! Why the fuck didn't you take a cab? Didn't think of it, said K lamely. But anyway, all that boring business is concluded now, and they get down to the business of drinking.

Financial Admin Man says that in Atlanta, where the band played two dates, they all stayed (minus the Rock Family, of course, from whom they were segregated as usual) on the 66th floor of a 72-storey hotel. He says the hotel some of them will be staying at in Seattle for two nights (where they stayed before) is built next to a lake stocked with carp and catfish and, K thinks he said, "sharks", and you are issued with fishing rods so you can fish from your room window if you want; and K mixes this up with the 72-storey hotel in Atlanta and gets rather a confusing picture.

What's the Stanhope like? K is asked by Dee.

My lips are sealed, replies K with a smile.

Dee winks; he knows the score.

They order another round of drinks: all on Dee's expenses.

What *really* happened to my predecessor, K asks Financial Admin Man, you know, the tutor on the Australian tour?

Oh, says Financial Admin Man airily, Buttercup was treating him like shit. He freaked out. Had to be bailed out of the tour.

This reminds Dee and Huey to return to the topic of bitching about life on tour, and then on to derisory remarks about the awful pianist/singer they are trying not to listen to, who has now embarked on a Richard Clayderman medley. A smartass New York type, is Dee's considered opinion. They are joined at the table by Financial Admin Man's Italian brother-in-law who has brought with him a friend, the captain of an Italian vessel now in port. Dee and Huey have gone on to wisecracking with the miniskirted waitresses, who don't seem to appreciate it much.

The bar has now closed, but Financial Admin Man nips upstairs and brings a bottle of Bourbon down from his room, and everyone's glass is topped up.

Where next?

Nassau, Long Island. A short trip, thank god, says Huey. You coming?

K explains he is not expected to attend gigs, the nature of his job being what it is. But the Head of Administration has promised to reserve him a complimentary ticket for Madison Square Garden, the final date of the East Coast phase of the tour.

A white-haired man alone at the corner table near them has fallen asleep in the dusk and begins to snore very loudly.

The pianist closes the lid of the piano softly, gets up and departs. The show is over.

•

In the morning, the bar area has been transformed: white tablecloths, napkins, gleaming cutlery. The guests, elderly couples mostly, are being served breakfast by elegant waiters foxtrotting between the tables bearing silver coffee-pots. Soothing music can just be discerned coming from hidden speakers. K has now taken to coming down for breakfast, having tired of room service (which also eats into his *per diem* more than somewhat). He rarely sees any other members of the tour party down here at this time. What he sometimes does is first nip out next door to a newsagent's to purchase for a dollar a copy of yesterday's *The Times* (that is, what they call here the *London Times*) so that he can catch up with the news from Britain over his buttered toast and coffee.

One waiter has lately befriended him. He's Irish. He saw K reading his newspaper one morning, and they fell to chatting about life in London, which the waiter had experienced for several years. While pouring the coffee, the Irish waiter saw he was reading the sports section, so the conversation turned to the English First Division, and the prospects for next season. The waiter said he kept up with the football via cable TV.

This morning, the friendly waiter approaches him with a coffee pot in one hand and a conspiratorial gleam in his eye.

See the fellow there, he says, don't look now but have a quick gander when you can, at that fellow with the beard.

He nods quickly in the general direction as he pours K's coffee.

K glances across with studied nonchalance. A solitary bearded man in a dark suit, breakfasting alone at a corner table, reading the *Wall Street Journal* with a frown.

You know who that is? That's John Erlichman, whispers the waiter.

John Erlichman?

You know, Nixon's henchman.

K knows. The man bears little resemblance to half-remembered images of former President Nixon's assistant and co-conspirator during the Watergate scandal. He recalls a clean-cut, clean-shaven WASPish Republican. He vaguely wonders what the man is doing out of jail.

K doesn't know – but finds out much later – that Erlichman is at this time awaiting the result of the appeal against his jail sentence, and in the meantime is whiling away the weeks by concluding a deal with a prominent New York publisher. That's for his novel *The Company*, which fictionalises the events leading up to Watergate, and is due to be published the following month. Some people have a genius for cashing in on an unpromising situation.

•

Madison Square Garden, twenty minutes till the band is due on stage. There's a hushed, even level of buzz, overlaying discreet baroque music playing over the house PA. The huge oval auditorium, like a grand circus, is ever so gradually filling up. Colours: muted oranges, yellows, greens, blues.

K is on his own, no-one sitting near him yet, to the left of the stage about ten yards back. These seats are reserved for the complimentaries. Kids wander around taking Polaroid flash snapshots of each other and of the stage. Red-coated ushers look bored. Press photographers take up crouching positions with their complicated cameras. On-stage: nine guitars ranged around variously, keyboard, sparkling drum-kit, tambourines hung on microphone stands, huge Marshall stacks.

Gradually, the seats next to K fill up. A surprisingly old, surprisingly straight bunch. Friends and family of the band. Business associates. A few straight guys in suits with and without beards who could be dead ringers for John Erlichman. Some children. Someone who turns out to be the head of the Rock Star's US fan club. The Head of Administration is there with a couple of other admin people. BB must be backstage. At the far end of the row, he can see Violet arriving with Buttercup and the little ones. He has brought two clandestine joints, but they stay in his pocket for the entire evening.

Then, just before the house lights go down, there is a small commotion in the audience. A bout of intense whispering. People crane their necks to look round, cameras pop, the press photographers quickly go into action mode. They close in on a lady with dark hair in a dark suit who has quietly appeared in the aisle with a small entourage; they take their places about ten rows behind where K is sitting. He recognises her as Jackie Kennedy Onassis.

On come the band, to a rapid crescendo of applause, plug in guitars, hook horns on their slings, adjust drums, Dee looks round to check everything is in order; and then the applause swells to a great roar as the Rock Star himself takes the stage, a spot following him, waving with both hands in acknowledgement. He straps on his instrument, and they launch straight into an instantly recognisable belter of an opening number.

The songs pour out. It's pretty slick, pretty well rehearsed. The Rock Star cannily mingles hits from his back catalogue – greeted with tumultuous applause from the first few notes – with numbers from the recently launched album. The sound is harder, tighter, more raucous than on the album. He moves to the keyboard. The ghost of everybody's youth lingers over the proceedings. He plays one of his biggest hits solo. More applause. Back on guitar, and meanwhile Dee, counting the band in when needed, is on bass now. The horn section hit their riffs perfectly in time, a moment of feedback on the trombonist's solo the only blemish. Wee Jimmy unleashes a stream of dirty euphoria from his guitar that was never on the record. You have to hand it to him. There are coloured lights, laser beams, a back-projected film, smoke-bombs on a climactic number. Everything's going at exactly the speed of sound for about two hours. The audience is bathed in a sufficiency of delight. But there are moments of stability too, when the churn subsides. An acoustic interlude, for instance, brings some spare space back into the thing – the darkened hall and a single spotlight – but not for too long, not enough to puncture that razzle, to allow forgetfulness; and before much time has elapsed it's back to that old rock'n'roll. Audience ecstatic, on their feet. Four encores. Cheers still ringing out with the band off the stage for the last time, even as most of the audience gradually begin to gather their belongings and file out along the aisles.

K is damned well impressed. He hasn't been too keen on the Rock Star's recent recordings, as compared with those classics from when he was in his pomp, but this is pretty good.

He can't see Violet or the kids any longer, nor the three or four people near him that he knows. Some have undoubtedly gone backstage. He decides to walk back to the hotel through the night along Manhattan's brightly-coloured streets, picking up a pastrami sandwich on the way. There is a small crowd of fans waiting patiently and hopefully by the porch of the St Regis. He takes the elevator to his room, gets ready for bed. In bed, while watching Johnny Carson in the *Tonight* show, he smokes one of the joints that was in his pocket.

•

Chicago! The Whitehall Plaza Hotel, East Delaware Place: a king-size bed with yellow sheets, large sunny picture window with orange drapes, TV and AM/FM radio, floor-length mirrors, private refrigerator. And the staff are distinctly more friendly and less stiff than at the St Regis. The bell-hop who takes K's bags up, a young lad, asks wonderingly if K is the Rock Star's manager.

K is here ahead of the rest of the party, and it's a marvel he has managed to pass the hotel security. He has been flown by United Airlines, LaGuardia to O'Hare. The others are all flying by private chartered jet. The Rock Star's family will, he has been told, be staying at a private house in the suburbs for the duration of this middle phase of the tour. How, where and how often he will be teaching Buttercup doesn't seem to have been decided. Violet, as usual, will not be domiciled with the family, and will be based here at the Whitehall Plaza with the rest, to be taken out daily to perform her domestic duties. Last night in the St Regis bar she confided to K that she too is unhappy and wants to make this her last tour.

Next day is a rest day, but it pours with rain, the kerbsides filling up with slush, the skies grey and misty. K whiles away the time by visiting the aquarium and planetarium, out on a limb exposed to Lake Michigan which is bedecked with mist and eerie with foghorns. Loses his way on the bus system on the return, dives into a hamburger joint to allay his hunger pangs, then finds the subway, which takes him back, wet and cold, to within walking distance of the hotel.

In the bar, which is as dusky with manufactured twilight as the St Regis one had been, he finds Financial Admin Man chatting merrily at a table with Wee Jimmy, the lead guitarist, who is with his girlfriend, and also Huey. They have been drinking a while. Financial Admin Man hails him and buys him a beer. Good gig at Madison Square Garden the other night, K comments to the musicians. Yeah, it was OK. It's been better. But Wee Jimmy is grumbling because he wants to have dinner in the hotel restaurant but they won't let him in without a tie. After a while, he and his girlfriend get up, Jimmy stating his intention of borrowing a necktie from someone, possibly BB, and they disappear; and soon after they are joined by Violet, who says she has also been to the aquarium and planetarium with some of the others. Sorry I didn't see you there, she says to K.

Over her third dry martini, late into the night, after even Financial Admin Man and Huey have gone up to bed, Violet confides to K: It's not a good life. The fame, she means, and its intrusion into family life. She has been with the family for years; in fact, has been employed by the Rock Star as a housekeeper since before his present marriage – originally brought in to clean his house for up to two hours daily; that was soon after her husband had died. She would like maybe to go back to just doing that. The kids seem fond of her, but she disapproves of their parenting. For instance, she is scandalised that the Rock Star and his wife don't seem to mind appearing nude in front of them. Buttercup is hard to manage. She has threatened several times to run away from home. Buttercup also has a hopeless crush on Wee Jimmy, which has caused some embarrassment. Violet has been a substitute mother for the kids for a few years now, she says, and considers she has been taken advantage of. She disapproves of the drug-taking too. And is contemptuous of BB – comparing him unfavourably to the Rock Star's previous manager – and of many of the other members of the organisation who she thinks are riding on a massive bandwagon. All of this pours out of her, unsolicited by K.

•

The sun is bright and high in the sky but Lake Michigan is the colour of a beer bottle and the waters look treacherously choppy. K is sitting on a stone ledge on a cobblestone beach watching people go by, on bikes, on foot, wearing sunny T-shirts. Behind him, on Lake Shore Drive, the traffic hums past. He is writing postcards home: to the people in the Share household in Sunderland Terrace, to Keith and Meryl, to his parents, his sister. He is, though, in a bad place.

He left a message with BB to ask what the arrangements would be for teaching Buttercup. And BB replied with a message saying a plan was being considered that he should be moved out of the Whitehall Plaza to a Holiday Inn out in the country, on his own, close to the residence where the family is staying, to "save expense".

K stared at this in shock. His heart sank to his shoes.

He contemplated the message for a very long time, pondering its implications.

This was ridiculous. In response, he wrote another note. He pushed it under BB's room door. The essence of the note was: No Way.

Now he has come out here to think.

•

BB acknowledged the note. Don't worry, he said to K on the phone, I'll sort this out. So for the present the arrangement is as before: he will be collected by limousine, along with Violet and bodyguard Jeff, and driven out each day to the farmhouse the family have rented. Except of course that this is not a question of a few blocks: it's an hour and a half's drive.

It's Memorial Day: a holiday. The Rock Star makes the morning news on NBC: the first concert in Chicago is coming up soon. He and his wife are interviewed, and they answer the reporter's inane questions politely, even interjecting some good-humoured quips, just like he did in the old days, on his first ever US tour. British humour, it goes down well.

At the farmhouse, as he arrives, the Rock Couple are on their way out. They greet K politely. K comments on how much he enjoyed the Madison Square Garden gig – that it really rocked. To his surprise, the Rock Star seems genuinely pleased with this assessment.

I'm really glad you thought that, he says. That's what we're trying to achieve: you know, at the bottom, we want it to be just a good little rocking band. Just like the old days.

Buttercup is in better humour than usual. She loves it here. The "farm" is actually a huge ranch-house overlooking miles of rolling fields. It is owned by the same millionaire who owns the Chicago Stadium, where the band will be playing. There are horses and ponies around, grazing. She is obsessed by them. Once she's said goodbye to her parents, she takes K out to look at them: That white one over there, that's an Arab, she says confidently.

An impressive golden-coloured animal trots up to the fence hoping for handouts.

That's a palomino.

They are proud frisky creatures, thinks K.

I love Appaloosas, she says, they're my favourite.

What are they like?

They're the ones that are spotty. You can't mistake them. They have one here, but he's in the stable.

The littler Rock Family children are brought out to play by Violet, and K challenges the elder one to a race across the field to the fence. There is hilarious scampering, and Violet smiles on benevolently.

He and Violet stand gazing around them at the extravagant house, at the fields extending to the horizon. The millions and millions of dollars they represent.

Nobody *earns* this, remarks Violet.

He knows what she means.

But to work, and Buttercup has to do a maths test today, to see how much she's taken in. Don't worry too much about it, reassures K, seeing her frowning face.

Why do I have to do maths?

We all need maths in life. For all sorts of reasons. Besides, you need at least basic maths for most jobs, so it will stand you in good stead.

I won't need a job, says Buttercup contemptuously. My dad's going to buy me a riding stable when I grow up. He promised me.

Is that so? Well, there you are then, Buttercup. You'll find maths useful for running that riding stable.

How's that?

Well, to do the accounts, and all that sort of thing.

Don't be silly, says Buttercup scornfully, I'll employ someone to do *that*.

The lesson is over. Buttercup has performed very moderately on the test. K tries to encourage her. She's still grizzling about it. Oh for goodness' sake Buttercup, please don't give me grief, it's only a bloody test, he says. She doesn't say any more.

It's 6pm, and by now the limousine should have come to pick him up. Just him, as Violet needs to stay on to look after the children. But half an hour goes by, and there's no sign of the car. K spends some time on the phone trying to get through to the hotel, and then to the limousine company.

They're very apologetic, but they don't have any instructions about picking him up. Eventually, it turns out BB forgot to let them know about this. Violet says this is typical.

He finally arrives back at the hotel, hungry, at 9.30, having promised Violet to ask the Whitehall barman to reserve her two dry martinis for when she is due to return at two in the morning.

The limousine driver, a grizzled veteran, is very jolly. He has driven many rock stars, he says, even the Rock Star himself on his very first US tour. That manager he used to have then, you remember, he passed away, he was a real gentleman.

He claims to have once driven Al Capone. You know, the biggest mobster there ever was, he adds unnecessarily for K's benefit. He employed sixty-three thousand people, can you imagine that? And the only reason he got put in jail was because he offended President Hoover.

K comments on the smoothness of the ride in this Cadillac. The driver says a lot of money is spent on its maintenance. He goes on to draw an elaborate analogy between the body of a car and the human anatomy, stressing the need to ingest oil with one's food. Your stomach's gotta have lubricant, he explains.

The rain comes on again.

On the TV news he's watching in bed, for some reason there are more legends of old Chicago. In 1923 apparently a street trader who owned a white horse thought he would drum up more business if the horse was transformed into a zebra. So he painted black stripes on it, and was later arrested for "defacing an animal". Before the trial, however, he was referred for medical reports to a unit for the criminally insane, where he remained without trial until his death in 1968.

Afterwards, K cannot make up his mind whether he actually heard this on the news or dreamt it.

•

K has a ticket for the big gig at Chicago Stadium. Violet is taking the kids too. So this afternoon K's lesson with Buttercup is cut short, and it makes sense for him to travel with them and with Jeff in the limousine, from the farmhouse straight to the venue. The kids chatter excitedly about it throughout the journey.

Chicago Stadium is a huge, ugly rectangular building, an ice-hockey arena normally holding around 14,000 spectators, but, Jeff says, expanded to 20,000 capacity for this gig. The limo drives up to the main gate, they are let through, and one minute later they are backstage.

Now Violet, Jeff and the kids are ushered to their seats in the front stalls. K's ticket, however, places him high up on the left of the stage. He is not too bothered about this.

The venue fills up to capacity, and what follows is a more or less exact rerun of the Madison Square Garden concert, with a very minimal tweak to the set list, but significantly worse sound quality and balance.

When the show ends, after the usual three or four encores, K decides he'd better wait for the others downstairs. The crowds are streaming out, but K catches sight of the three children being shepherded in the direction of the backstage area, under the always watchful eye of Jeff. They are showing their stage passes. He catches Buttercup's eye across the temporary barrier; she beckons him to join them, but he explains to her over the hubbub that he has never been issued with a pass. She promises to tell Financial Admin Man that he is waiting outside, before Jeff comes over to gently move her on.

K waits, as the crowds melt away into the night, but nothing happens. The police are beginning to move all the stragglers on. He talks to one of the officers, explains his position, asks if he can send through a message backstage. A young man in a denim jacket whom K vaguely recognises overhears the conversation. Can I help? he says. His name is Barry; he is a PR man for the Rock Star's US record label. Sure, he tells K, I'll take a message in to Financial Admin Man. He disappears. Two or three minutes later, he comes back apologetically with the return message that Financial Admin Man has said there's no transportation laid on, and K will need to take a taxi.

K makes his way out onto the street in what is now a blind rage. All the snubs, all the pettiness, the paranoia, everything, it all mounts into a crescendo in his brain. His hands are sweating. Young people are milling around, some congregating and making a great hubbub around the artists' gate. K sees the limousines pull out, one by one.

There are no taxis to be had anywhere. A cop tells him he thinks they would all avoid the area if they had any sense. He walks on, not knowing quite where he is going. The large crowd has vanished magically into the night; the stadium lights are now out of vision. There are dark streets ahead. It looks pretty rough, all of a sudden. Perhaps if he can find the next major road intersection, that will tell him which direction to head in.

Someone emerges from the shadow of a side street, calls out to him. He makes out what appears to be a youngish black man. The man is not threatening, but appears to be offering him something. He calls back in his best British accent: No, I'm all right, thanks!

Surely there will be taxis at that next main intersection coming up. Ahead, he can see a small group of uniformed police officers outlined against a street lamp beside a parked squad car. The elevated railway looms overhead. He approaches the cops cautiously. They turn. Again, he asks where he can find a taxi to the Whitehall Plaza Hotel. In East Delaware Place.

Two of the cops look at each other, then at him. East Delaware, yeah. They are white. They seem to be Irish-American from the way they speak. They finger their holsters. They are big guys, but they actually seem nervous. That's the impression he gets, anyway. I wouldn't go any further if I were you, one advises him, finally. The other says: Just stay here with us, and wait for a bus. There'll be one along here taking you near East Delaware before too long.

So he waits, while the cops continue a desultory conversation among themselves.

Five minutes later, a car pulls up, a big Oldsmobile. To his amazement, the driver is Barry, the record company PR guy who took his message backstage. He leans out of the window. You still having a problem? he calls. Never mind, I can give you a lift, jump in.

K is hugely relieved. The cops watch impassively, then turn away, continuing to finger their holsters.

That's a very bad neighbourhood, around the stadium, explains Barry as he drives. A very bad neighbourhood. Don't worry, I'll take you to the hotel. It's a heck of a way, actually.

He suggests they might smoke some dope on the ride, but can't find his stash in the dashboard compartment. K is getting worried again, but, as an enticement to Barry, he mentions he has some grass in his hotel room. So when– to K's great relief – they pull up outside the Whitehall Plaza at last, he keeps his word, runs up to his room and fetches his stash. By now, he has figured out Barry is a good guy.

So Barry drives them around for an hour as they smoke K's joint. He shows him the plush suburbs reposing with their twinkling lights down by the Lake. A different world. It's beautiful. They chat. It's nice, K has calmed down. He tells Barry about the tour, and how he got involved with it, and how he now wishes he hadn't. Barry lives in Chicago; he has been working with the East Coast stage of the operation throughout, which is why he was a familiar face to K, but this is the end of the tour for him – tomorrow he goes back to plugging records, this time in Milwaukee.

Barry deposits him back at the hotel once more, and K thanks him profusely. No problem, says Barry, and drives off into the night.

On the way in, he notices Financial Admin Man holding court over a bunch of guys in the bar, where there is much drunken hilarity, but he doesn't feel like talking. He goes up to his room, orders a club sandwich from room service and goes to bed. He doesn't wake up until 10.30 in the morning.

•

BB is not available. K learns he is spending time out at the farm. They say he is taking a lot of stick from the Family. The Head of Administration is not available, perhaps not even here any longer. Someone said they'd seen her in tears. Clearly, K doesn't know the half of what is going on. Violet is sorry for him, and gives him a bunch of official tour T-shirts (he's happened to mention to her he was told he "wasn't entitled" to have one). The guys in the band are always cheery when he sees them. Except Wee Jimmy, where is he? Sources say he is on the verge of being thrown out of the tour by the Rock Star. Apparently, he has had a row with his girlfriend and sent her packing and is now hitting the booze heavily, which the Rock Star will not like at all. It did seem his solos at the Chicago Arena were a bit subdued compared to those at Madison Square Garden, but maybe that's hindsight. Financial Admin Man has a bad cold and constantly gets paralytically drunk. The official tour photographer has resigned and gone home to England, after a disagreement, it's said, with the Rock Couple.

Then K gets a communication from BB, but it's not what he wanted at all. After a day at the beach and at Chicago Zoo by himself, he returns to the hotel in the early evening to find a note from BB in his room, to the effect that he is required to move to a hotel a couple of blocks away from here for the final two nights in Chicago. No reason given, except that it is of the Utmost Importance. He is to ring a number, which is that of a man called Mark, who works for the tour promoters. K calls the number, Mark answers, K states categorically that he has no intention of moving. This Mark is embarrassed, doesn't know what to say to him. Says he honestly doesn't know the reason for the move, he's just been asked to implement a decision. K ends the call, dashes off a blistering reply to BB, and posts the note under BB's room door.

Later in the evening, BB comes round to K's room. He is looking a bit bleary eyed. He says he needs to explain. K lets him in.

BB is standing by the window, occasionally glancing out, a bit fidgety. He's in a dark suit with an open shirt collar. K has flung himself on the bed, propped up against the pillows.

So what is this all about? demands K. I thought we'd agreed I wasn't going to be stuck in a hotel on my own out in the sticks just to save a bit of money. Now this is a hotel two blocks away from here that you want to put me in? What's the sense in that?

I understand, says BB, I understand your frustration. We're all trying to cope with some difficult situations.

Well, this is a truly difficult situation I'm in now, shouts K, I've never been in a more difficult situation.

To his own dismay, he finds his voice faltering, he is on the verge of tears, something that hasn't happened for a very long time. He must control himself, he thinks, he can't be showing weakness to this man. But BB has already sensed this anyway; his eyes flick away to the night scene outside the window, then back again to K. There is a hint of compassion in his face.

No, this isn't about saving money, says BB. It's about a ruling we've had.

From the Rock Couple, he means.

It's a ruling that the household staff and the band should not stay at the same hotel. They're very concerned to keep their private and work lives separately. As you know.

Household staff? So is Violet being asked to move too?

No, she isn't.

K is about to ask why not, but the question dies in his mouth: of course, Violet is untouchable, she's been with the Rock Star too long, so they wouldn't dare demand of her this further step. It's bad enough requiring her to be a surrogate mother to the kids yet have to be bussed out each day to do that job. So, essentially, for this purpose, "household staff" is a category comprising just one individual: himself.

K changes what he was going to say: This is a terrible way to communicate, he manages to blurt.

I know, I know. (BB spreads his hands helplessly.)

I tried to contact the Head of Administration to find out what was going on, but she wasn't available.

BB's eyes flicker again. He is standing with his back to the window now.

The Head of Administration has gone to Vancouver for a few days' rest, he says, after a pause. Where she has some family and friends. Anyway, to get back to this matter.

What?

Can I please ask you to move to the other hotel just for the last night in Chicago? Then we can review the situation for the final phase of the tour.

K thinks.

OK, he says. One night.

I appreciate that, says BB, visibly relieved.

When he has gone, K gets ready for bed. He thinks about his options. He is determined to tell the Rock Star tomorrow what he feels about all this. But that may be the end of the tour for him. So be it.

Next day, he and Violet are as usual taken by limo all the way out to the farm. On the way, he tells Violet about what's happened. Violet is sympathetic. No, she hasn't been asked to move. No, she confirms that would be a step too far in her case.

They arrive at the farmhouse. K is nervous. The Rock Couple are around, and they are unusually friendly to him, even jovial. Would you like some iced tea? asks the Rock Star. His wife has just made some in the kitchen, and she pours K out a glass from the jug, ice cubes clinking. Just the thing for these warm mornings, she says. Yes, it's turning hot at last.

Carrying his iced tea, K moves towards the room that has been designated for Buttercup's schooling – where they have only managed two or three lessons in the ten days they have been in Chicago – and the Rock Star follows him in. Just one thing before I fetch Buttercup, says the Rock Star. Here it comes, K thinks, here's the discussion about this business. He braces himself.

Only, I was just talking to Buttercup yesterday, and she says you swore at her.

He wasn't expecting this.

I swore at her? K is aghast. I wouldn't swear at a pupil.

Then to his consternation he recalls: that "bloody" that escaped his lips! When he said to her, what was it, "it's only a bloody test". Can it be that?

Well, that's what Buttercup said, continues the Rock Star. He has a fixed smile on his face as he stares at K, nodding slightly. So I thought I should tell you.

I didn't swear at her, K lies, but all the fight has gone out of him now.

I just thought I'd let you know, says the Rock Star again. What she said. I wouldn't appreciate it, of course. Swearing at my daughter.

I didn't, I wouldn't.

OK, he says. He leaves the room, saying he needs to get ready for that night's gig in St Paul, Minnesota; and Buttercup enters, a little sullen as usual.

No more is said about this. About anything, really.

•

The taxi driver hired to take K from his new hotel – the Water Tower Hyatt, where he has spent a single night – to O'Hare Airport is a young kid, starry-eyed. K is wearing the official black T-shirt with the tour logo.

You with the tour? Yeah? Wow! Wow!! the exclamation marks proliferate in his voice. I was there the other night at the Chicago Arena! Dynamite show!

It was pretty good, wasn't it, says K, smiling indulgently in the back of the cab.

Dynamite show!! So where you going next?

We're flying to LA where we're based for the last stage of the tour. Gigs in Denver, Seattle, San Francisco, San Diego, Tucson....

WOW!!!

As before, K is booked into a United Airlines flight on his own. Three hours later, he is high over the Mojave Desert, having cruised over the Painted Desert and the Grand Canyon. Starting the descent to Los Angeles. Tiny puffy clouds drifting below across the azure space.

It has been decided that K will not after all be booked into the Beverly Wilshire Hotel, as promised at the start of the tour, where the rest of the party, including Violet, are to be based. Instead, he will be on his own at the Holiday Inn, Beverly Hills, situated several blocks up Wilshire Boulevard.

He is past caring. On arrival, anyway, he finds his reservation has been made, and he checks in. His room is about half the size of the ones he has become accustomed to, but adequate for his needs. There is no refrigerator, but a Coca Cola machine on the landing outside dispenses that beverage, not in cans but in the original, green-tinted bottles. The TV in the room works well enough after you have smacked it on the side. The maids are invisible, only leaving their mark in the form of the traditional tape sealing the toilet seat. There are no mint chocolates on the pillow. No "just checking" visits, thank god, and no turning down the bed covers, you have to do that yourself. Room service is limited. There is a small rooftop pool for the benefit of guests.

Sunday morning. Sunshine – though it has rained. Nothing to do. He walks out onto Wilshire Boulevard. Decides to explore. Unbelievably spindly palm trees, tall as the vapour trails of sky-rockets, line the wide road at intervals. Skyscraper bank buildings behind them. He turns northward, crosses Santa Monica Boulevard, eventually hits the brash come-ons of the Sunset Strip. A cinema is showing a double bill of *Shampoo*, starring Warren Beatty, and *Robin and Marian*, with Sean Connery and Audrey Hepburn as the eponymous duo, so he pays his money and goes in to while away three or four hours. Terrible films, what a waste. Out in the sunshine again, heads west, walks past the elegant Spanish-styled houses of Beverly Drive: arches, wrought-iron gates, patios, white walls, shutters, the scent of conifers and flowers in full bloom. And more Rolls Royces than he has seen in his entire lifetime.

Suddenly, he notices a pair of armed cops, or maybe they are private security guards, watching him intently from afar, and he becomes hyper-aware that he is the *only person walking* in this neighbourhood, which is not good. He hurries on, trying not to seem as though he is hurrying, thankfully hits Wilshire Boulevard again. And there it is across the road, the Beverly Wilshire, like a castle, fronted by its imposing blond portico where the taxis line up, all surmounted by huge Stars & Stripes flags limp on their staffs. So that's it, that's where the rest of the tour party will be staying.

A few blocks back up Wilshire, and there's the Holiday Inn. Hunger pangs return. He decides to try the Gaucho Steak

House. As in so many similar establishments, the lighting is so dim here that he cannot read his copy of yesterday's *Times*, purchased at a newsstand on Hollywood Boulevard, not even from three inches away; also, it is almost deserted. There is nobody to talk to. He decides to forego the steak and orders instead scampi and rice, with a glass of Burgundy. The waitresses flounce around, wearing almost non-existent miniskirts. A wave of unbearable sexual frustration hits him. And also he is homesick. He is thinking about Marie. What will she be doing now? He has sent her a postcard, addressed to Sunderland Terrace, separately from the one he sent to the general household.

More wine? asks one of the waitresses, seeing his glass empty. Beautiful smile. She has a ring on her left third finger, ah, she's married. He declines.

Time to go up to his room and watch some TV. See if there's a baseball game on. If not, there's the jazz station, KBCA 105.1.

The sky has started to darken outside now, and a floodlit American Bicentennial flag undulates very slightly atop the Glendale Federal building. The traffic on Wilshire has calmed considerably. Down the corridor the Coke and ice machines hum, the elevator clanks.

•

The California primaries are on. TV adverts at considerable volume constantly plug the virtues of the various shiny-teethed candidates in this glorious bicentennial year in which America has touched eternity over and over. They walk into halls in a triumphant blare of music. Balloons, placards and buttons. Red, white and blue. Miss America is nothing compared to this. Smiling replaces dialectic. Electronic micro-organisms infiltrate the lush infrastructures of the public consciousness at every level. Money follows its own rules of discourse, and the deep throat of the public gags for more. But it's almost all sewn up by now: on the red side, which confusingly is what the rest of the world regards as blue, certainly so; on the blue (red) side very nearly so. Then the next level up: the real fight will be on, but actually it all takes place in hyperreality.

•

So now, the arrangement for this final phase of the tour is as follows: K is to wait by his phone at the Holiday Inn each morning for the call, ideally before noon, that will tell him the agenda for that day. Either he will receive a message saying his services are not required, and he is then free for the rest of the day; or he will be informed that there is to be a lesson at such and such a time, in which case the limousine will first collect Violet at the Beverly Wilshire, pick him up on the way (he is to wait outside the Holiday Inn), and they will be then taken to the mystery location where the Family are lodging. The limousine will pick him up and deliver him back to the Holiday Inn when the lesson is finished.

And so it comes to pass on Monday. The huge white Cadillac limousine draws up outside the Holiday Inn, and K, who has been waiting at the kerb, gets in and joins Violet. The limo driver is one of the silent ones.

The car takes a right, and enters a complex of winding roads, climbing higher and higher into the Hollywood Hills. The morning is clear, without a cloud in the sky above, though there's a haze on the horizon. As they negotiate the bends, there are occasional views between the pine trees of Beverly Hills and Los Angeles spread out and glittering below them. The HOLLYWOOD sign is clearly visible.

They arrive at a pair of wrought iron gates, which swing open slowly and mysteriously to let the car in and onto the gravel drive where it parks. Violet gets out and pulls the bell on the enormous carved wooden front door, which is opened by a smiling black woman in a maid's uniform. They go through into the dim entrance hall. There is daylight, though, ahead.

The house is a magnificent Spanish style structure perched atop a hill. A hacienda, they call it. Violet has been here before. She says it was formerly owned by Howard Hughes and is now the property of Hugh Hefner. It is built around a central patio or atrium with a roof that can be slid to cover the whole space, but is currently retracted. In the centre of the patio is a small, brilliant blue swimming pool. Glass sliding doors surround this space on all four sides, leading to the various rooms. Everything is open-plan, with unpolished wood, exposed brickwork and red tiles featuring heavily.

The Rock Couple are in their swimsuits sitting by the pool. They greet Violet like a long-lost friend. The Rock Wife has numerous urgent domestic matters to discuss with her, which occupies everyone for some minutes while K waits. The maid is bustling around meanwhile. Her name seems to be Tommy. Buttercup appears, golden haired, in shorts, flip-flops and a T-shirt. K is shown into the grand living room, opening off the patio, in a corner of which is a desk at which the lessons will take place. In another corner the floor is covered by a vast polar-bearskin rug. Buttercup grimaces at this. In a third corner is a pool table.

After the lesson is over – by which time the Rock Couple have departed, probably in the same limousine that delivered Violet and K – heading for the plane to Denver, which is tonight's gig – K challenges Buttercup to a game of pool. She beats him comprehensively. She enjoys that. They are all laughs and smiles as his limo arrives to take him back.

•

He exits the Holiday Inn in the early evening sunshine, deciding to walk the three or four blocks down to the Beverly Wilshire. He needs to touch base with Financial Admin Man about his *per diem* expenses for the week ahead.

A girl is waiting outside the lobby, shyly. She is maybe sixteen or seventeen years old, who can tell. She calls out to him: Hi.

Hi, he returns, stopping momentarily in his tracks.

She's lovely, wearing cut-off jeans, blonde hair. Beautiful, blue-eyed smile.

Hi, are you with the tour?

He forgot he was wearing the T-shirt, of course.

I might be.

And the next question will be of course: does he know, can he tell her, where the Rock Star and his family are staying in Hollywood?

He could spin this out a little, if he has the street-wisdom, the quickness of thought. He could for instance say: well, let's meet for a drink, and we can talk about it. We can talk about what I know and what I don't know. But most of these thoughts tend to only formulate themselves after the event, when it's too late.

How is it she's latched onto the Holiday Inn? He is, as far as he knows, the only tour member lodged there. Everyone who knows anything at all will know the bulk of the party is at the Wilshire. And before long they will all know about the house in the Hills anyway, but they don't yet. And he is honour bound. Stupid. Honour bound. Ho ho. But he could say to her, well, I can't tell you that information right now, how about meeting for a drink. You know, the room service is pretty good, I admit it's not the Beverly Wilshire, but I am lodged here for specific reasons which I can tell you about. And you dig this T-shirt? it's the official tour T-shirt not available to the general public you know, but I think I have a spare that might just be your size, would you like it? And then later when he is fucking her to kingdom come on his Holiday Inn bed, maybe in the most extreme throes of his ecstasy he might just shout out the address of the house in the hills "inadvertently", so that would be the let-out for him if so. That he didn't mean to do it. That would be understandable. How beautiful she is, and how eager.

But the honey girl is nervous, grins again prettily.

I'm sorry, says K in his British accent, I don't think I can help you.

Oh, no problem, sorry to bother you, she says.

And he turns and continues on his way, but he's thinking to himself fuck it fuck it, you blew it you stupid fucking idiot.

For the official T-shirt, especially when inhabited by a British accent, opens doors everywhere. A ticket office on Beverly Drive: Hey, are you on the tour? Vigorous handshake. Real pleased to meet him. A man in maybe his forties, in a baseball cap, very affable. Why, his name is K too. Fancy that. Seems to know more about the tour than he, K, the original K, does. Like, he may be going to the end-of-tour party, to which over eight hundred people have been invited, apparently. Can you believe that? I guess you're going?

K says he very well might be, though this is the first he has heard of such a party. A tacit pretence of knowledge seems the safest strategy here anyway.

So what are you after here? asks the other K, indicating the ticket counter.

Thinking about going to that concert at the Burbank Starlight Bowl, K tells him, the headliners being Weather Report and Grover Washington. He really wants to see Weather Report.

Hey, I can get you a ticket. No problem.

Another middle-aged man in the queue, sorry, the line, has been buying tickets for the Rock Star's upcoming Los Angeles Forum gig, he says. For his kids, he says. He couldn't help overhearing. Hey, would you mind signing the back of the tickets, he says sweetly. For the kids. Certainly, smiles K.

How it feels to be on the fringe of the insanity.

But how easy is it to get to the Starlight Bowl in Burbank? The first man, the other K, the double, says to come with him, and takes him down the road to yet another dimly lit restaurant where his secretary, who as it happens lives in Burbank, is waiting for him, and she writes down comprehensive instructions – which assume, of course, that he is in possession of a motor car.

•

The Beverly Wilshire lobby is like the hushed entrance to a cathedral – yes, dimly lit of course, but with this difference, the pile of the plum carpet covering the vast floor from wall to wall is so thick you have great difficulty wading through.

Financial Admin Man was not available yesterday evening, but said he would be there this morning, so K has left a message with the authorities that he will be at the Wilshire if required to do his job today.

Financial Admin Man is to be discovered, of course, in the bar, drinking with a very attractive and smartly dressed woman who turns out to be from the Rock Star's US record label. Hi, she says sweetly. Yes, she knows Barry very well, she says in answer to K's question, but K does not elaborate on how he came to meet Barry. Propped up on a vacant chair beside them is the cover of the most recent LP, not the studio album they are promoting on this tour but a repackaged compilation of the Rock Star and his cohorts' previous successes.

It's already shipped platinum, she announces proudly, lapsing into record company argot.

They marvel at this for some moments.

When the attractive lady has gone, Financial Admin Man, who is a little bleary round the eyes, says he has a few minutes to attend to K's expenses. Come with me, he commands. So K follows him through the gloom out into the bright sunshine of the outdoor pool area. It is a large swimming pool, bigger than the Holiday Inn rooftop one, surrounded by a spacious, tiled sunbathing area – two or three guests are taking advantage – and Financial Admin Man's room, quite a dinky one, is one of several that conveniently open straight out onto this. K sits on a candy-striped director's chair while Financial Admin Man goes indoors to rummage about and fetch the cash.

The dollar bills are counted out, the travel expense chits collected. Fuck me, are you *still* riding buses? exclaims Financial Admin Man. In LA?

There are buses here, believe it or not, says K. I find them quite convenient actually.

K is in shorts. He stretches his legs out. The sunlight pours down on them.

It's great here, isn't it?

You could come and sunbathe, I guess.

Yeah, it's better than the Holiday Inn.

Although it's strictly against company rules, ho ho, adds Financial Admin Man.

But K's brief comfort is interrupted when suddenly his name is called over the tannoy.

Is that me? Christ.

It's BB who wants him. The call has just come through that there's to be a lesson this afternoon. BB is in the lobby. He himself has also been summoned to the presence of the great one for a meeting, and suggests sharing a limo. The idea is that he will be finished within the hour and will return imminently, but will arrange for another limo to pick K up when his lesson with Buttercup is over.

But this is not what happens. K can hear the low hum of BB's and the Rock Star's voices in conversation outside in the hacienda's open area, as a backdrop for the entirety of Buttercup's lesson and their subsequent game of pool. Mostly he can hear the Rock Star's voice; there is a nagging insistency about it. Then BB's low, measured voice has its own interlude, but is quickly interrupted. The Rock Star is clearly not happy. There is some problem that evidently cannot easily be fixed.

Violet is not around today. The maid, Tommy, wants to slip away, and asks K for Violet's number at the Wilshire. K's limousine arrives. Cautiously, he interrupts the Rock Star and BB, but having been in discussion for over two hours they are still not finished, so he rides home on his own. It's the chatty limo driver this time; he spends most of the drive telling K about all the other famous people he drives, including most recently Telly Savalas.

•

The preacher is black, middle-aged, hair grizzling and receding a little at the sides. How and when he appeared at the Holiday Inn is unclear. He is clad mainly in a diaphanous, flowing vestment of a sky-blue colour; indeed, it's like the Californian sky has descended onto and partly draped itself around him, only the bottoms of his dark trousers and shiny black shoes being visible. He glides, he is solemn and evidently benevolent. Preacher? But he doesn't actually preach – more like intones. Maybe a prophet. As he comes out of the elevator and moves along the corridors of the hotel, he is sometimes accompanied by a female assistant; she is slightly younger than him, with tight but natural hair, wearing a white robe.

Sometimes they are chanting in a low tone – the hymn-like tune can barely be discerned – and sometimes mumbling what sounds, from the repetitive rhythms of the language, like prayers. Once he was observed standing on the pavement outside the hotel entrance, his arms outstretched to the sky above Wilshire Boulevard, in silent contemplation. At other times he is encountered wandering from table to table in the hotel restaurant, chanting and giving his blessing to the diners while his wife (if that's what she is) tags along behind him carrying a bible or a prayer book – a black leather-bound book, anyway – and singing in sweet harmony. When he approaches, you can see his eyes are a pale grey, and he has a cast – both eyes do not quite look in the same direction, one of them at you, the other perhaps in the direction of eternity. Does God care about you? he asks each diner, but the question is rhetorical, he answers it himself: yes, he does! yes, he does!

Then two days later, just as abruptly as he appeared in the hotel, he is gone, and seen no more.

•

Another apparition. It is a very hot June day; K has decided to take the bus all the way down to Santa Monica Beach. It turns out to be as wide as the Sahara. Roller-skating occurs on the fringes of it, under the palms. A swim in the Holiday Inn or even the Wilshire pool might be a better idea after all, so he turns back without ever reaching the ocean. He finds his bus terminates at the bus terminal, so he will have to change there. Stepping down, he sees a large crowd has assembled, under powerful lights. There is a film crew. And who should he see next but Telly Savalas himself, in a shiny blue-grey suit and black homburg, having his face dabbed with makeup. The crowd is told to hush and not to take flash pictures while shooting is in progress. K knows something the crowd does not: who the limo driver was who last drove the TV star. He has also now learnt that the detective series in which he features, one of his favourite programmes, is not after all shot in gritty New York, where it is set, but in Hollywood. So then Telly Savalas disappears behind a pair of glass swing doors, on command reappears as Lt Kojak, followed by his assistant Crocker, played by Kevin Dobson; "accidentally" bumps into a woman, who drops the case she was carrying as a result; he picks it up and hands it politely back to her, and a short dialogue ensues. But the director is clearly not quite satisfied, because he orders the scene to be re-shot. Almost exactly the same thing happens. Then again, a third take. They go through the same brief procedure four or five times, before there is a mumbled conference, and someone shouts "Lunch!" The crowd slowly starts to disperse.

•

Apparition number three: at 1.45am on a TV show called "Midnight Special", Bo Diddley shows up, playing classical music on solo violin, rather ably.

•

Weather Report are magnificently exciting at the Starlight Bowl in Burbank on Saturday night, K thinks. The open-air amphitheatre is well filled. As dusk falls, searchlights pan slowly across the sky, onstage blues and golds deepening, then dissolving to greens and reds with white spotlights. The veteran jazzer John Handy is the opening act, on alto, with his son playing drums in the band.

There is a false start to Weather Report's set, due to a problem with one of Joe Zawinul's keyboards, but once they get off into a groove all goes well: jagged, haunting, fierce music, Wayne Shorter playing mainly soprano sax, extended skirmishes between the percussion and the drum kit, and a waywardly flamboyant new bass player taking solos whose name, K learns, is Jaco Pastorius.

So K is well pleased with his decision to make the effort to catch this. There have been several fallow days. The whole party decamped to Seattle for two nights, no doubt staying at that hotel with the angling facilities, so once again he was left to his own devices. And then on their return, he's been waiting vainly by the phone all morning; finally manages to get through to Jeff who says now the family are going to the Tucson gig, wasn't he told, no, there will be no lesson today either. Oh fuck it, Burbank tonight for him.

But he's beginning to worry. As Weather Report's set comes to a close, he becomes aware the whole thing is running well behind time. He arrived on a bus, and now realises he's probably about the only person in the audience who did so. They will stop running soon, he knows. It might be best, after all, to miss the headline act, Grover Washington, whom he's not quite so interested in, and start heading back.

Getting out of the auditorium is one thing, but when he reaches the bus stop at which he arrived he realises to his dismay that it's now 11pm and the buses stopped running a while ago. Nor is there a cab in sight.

Flashbacks to the Chicago Stadium.

He walks a mile down to the nearest main drag, Glenoaks, in downtown Burbank, but even there no cab is available to be hailed. Walking all the way back to Wilshire is out of the question: we are talking miles and miles, he sees, consulting his map, and that seems to include negotiating several freeways; he could spend the rest of his life in the attempt.

Stupid, stupid.

Though that could be a short life. Some drunken seventeen-year-old white punks waiting at another bus stop for non-existent buses provide a hint of menace. One of them latches onto K, spoiling for a confrontation. Why are you carrying a purse, man? he barks, pointing. It is K's shoulder bag he is alluding to. K does not reply. Hey guys, says the youngster, trying to engage his peer group, this guy's got a *purse*! But the rest of the gang aren't interested in the issue of the shoulder bag, having some arguments of their own to deal with. K decides to cross the road at that point and to enquire about cabs at the all-night supermarket he has seen. He is given a number, and calls it at the nearby payphone. Mercifully, there is a reply. He describes his location, and where he wants to go.

While he's waiting for the cab to arrive, another Burbank kid approaches. Hey man, are you over 21? he demands.

In full paranoia mode now, K gives him the brush-off, though it turns out all this young man wants is for someone to buy liquor for him at the store.

Miraculously, the cab arrives, and takes him all the way to the Holiday Inn for sixteen bucks.

•

Buttercup is interrupted while playing pool with a small blond English guy. She's a good couple of inches taller than he. Putting his cue up: You're too good for me, Buttercup, he says with a smile. She introduces him to K, this is Adam, she says. Hello, Adam. Pleased to meetcha, he says. They shake hands politely.

As she's showing him out, Violet tells K in an elaborate pantomime, whispering between clenched teeth: That's *Adam Faith!*

K meditates on the presence of yet another legend.

Buttercup is actually grumpier than usual throughout her lesson. Violet says later she's upset because Wee Jimmy has found a new girlfriend.

The lesson thankfully over, K emerges to find the Rock Star in swimming trunks sitting by the pool strumming an acoustic guitar. It is very hot out here. The Rock Star smiles winningly at him. Your tan is coming on, he says. He comments favourably on the leather belt K has acquired in one of the posh shops in Beverly Hills. He jokes that K is rapidly turning Californian.

While they're waiting for the limo, K suggests another game of pool with Buttercup. While they play, he can hear the Rock Star outside, singing in a sweet baritone that is recognisable but quite different from his rock voice: *Besame, besame mucho*, he croons, his fingers strumming an accompanying bossa rhythm.

K and Buttercup haven't been playing their game long before her father calls out to them. But it's not the car arriving; he wants to show Buttercup a tight formation of light aircraft that has appeared in the blue sky above the house trailing an advertising message of some sort. Buttercup cheers up. K brings out his Instamatic and takes a snapshot of the planes. Buttercup says she has a great idea, why doesn't her dad hire a skywriter plane to trail the tour strapline over an open-air concert on their next tour. The Rock Star says he will think about that. As they are both gazing skyward, on an impulse K turns his camera on them and snaps them both. But that may have been a faux pas. The Rock Star darts a quick look at him. Nothing is said, but.

There are fine lines one may not cross.

That may have been the last lesson, anyway.

The limo arrives.

This heat doesn't let up. His duties done, K decides to use the Beverly Wilshire swimming pool for a swim. What can it matter now?

The avenue swelters. Outside the big hotel's forecourt, dozens of elderly folk, all carrying flowers, are waiting for taxis. An incongruously scarlet-coated, top-hatted commissionaire moves among the bellhops who are darting about toting stacks of luggage and the security men and limo drivers who are standing around chatting.

Out of the hotel comes a handsome, brown-suited, sunglassed man who can only be Warren Beatty. He gets into one of the limos and it drives off.

Violet has left a further pile of official and unofficial tour T-shirts for him. It's a little act of defiance on her part, which he finds touching. He'll use them as presents for friends.

He has survived.

Two attractive girls sunbathing by the poolside nudge each other when he walks by.

He dines alone on hamburger steak, iced tea and cheesecake.

He has an attack of insomnia, waking in the hot night and worrying about his future. There is no job to go to after this ends. And maybe no home. He has not heard anything from Sunderland Terrace. Or from Marie. Puts on the light to read. Then he falls into a dream-torn sleep. He has decided to go on an expedition to the beach. But it lies beyond a lush forest. The only people he knows have disappeared. The beach, when he reaches it, is deserted, waves mash against some rocks. That is the end of the world. He decides to pitch camp about half a mile from the sea. He hears the howling of wolves, but nothing molests him. He sees a house nearby that he hasn't noticed before: it has a placard outside saying it is for rent. He decides to take it, but when he enters he finds he is, after all, back home. Though there is much that is unfamiliar about it. Then his father appears through a doorway and points out an enormous aquarium that has appeared in the middle of the room they are in, filled with beautiful, multi-coloured fish. But the water level is dropping rapidly. He tries to point this out, to no avail. His father is no longer there. And now, just as the water has become dangerously shallow, the tank starts to fill up again, and he realises this is a natural, cyclical process, and he is very relieved.

Are you going to the Forum gig? someone, possibly Financial Admin Man's assistant, asks him while he is waiting for his last lot of expenses to be worked out.

The gig at the LA Forum will be the grand finale of the tour of America. Among the guests expected in the audience are rumoured to be Ringo Starr, Elton John and Cher.

No, he doesn't think so, he's not that much bothered.

He doesn't receive an invitation to the end of tour party either, but he didn't want to go anyway. What would he do there?

It's all OK, he survived, that's the main thing. What's the point in getting uptight? It doesn't mean a lot. Regrets, well, he's had a few, but then again. What a fucking ninny he was, almost bursting into tears because he's going to be moved from one posh hotel to a different, slightly less posh one.

It doesn't mean a thing. None of it does.

Violet has promised to invite him over to the Rock Star's London home for a cup of tea while the family are away in Scotland, which is their next plan. In the event, that never happens.

BB is taking his family to Hawaii as soon as his work on the tour is finished. Dee will be going to Boston. Wee Jimmy is staying on in the States too, with his brother and sister-in-law, and perhaps his new girlfriend. It will be three years before his brother finds him dead in his flat in London, of heart failure due to alcohol poisoning. The American horn section are all going back to their respective homes, and Jane, the Head of Administration's assistant in the Rock Star's London office, who turned up for the LA stage of the tour, is planning to live with Steve, the trumpeter. As for the Head of Administration, K has not spoken to her since New York, though he thinks he spotted her once, from afar, at the Beverly Wilshire.

The candidates for the Presidential election later this year have now been selected, according to the TV news. There is shouting, flag-waving, singing, weeping. America is great again. And again.

The Glendale Building Bicentennial flag is limp this evening. There is still a faint cream glow on the western horizon, and the lights of the cars move slowly up and down Wilshire Boulevard. It's the end of another working week.

•

He's on the TWA flight home, LA International to Heathrow, via the North Pole. Banks of dark-blue cloud outside the porthole stretching to a pink horizon. The rest of the party are due to fly tomorrow. He convinces himself that the man sitting in front of him – they are each occupying a double seat at the back of the plane – is the Traffic drummer Jim Capaldi. Dead spit. He heard him speak to the stewardess, he has a British accent. But why would a famous rock star like him be flying second-class? It's not as if he's a tutor. At one point, the man borrows the headphones from the vacant seat next to him to watch the movie, as his own are not working, he says. The man doesn't comment on the tour T-shirt he is wearing. He tries to get some sleep.

•

So it might have been thought that when K arrived at long last back home at Sunderland Terrace, and was greeted by some familiar faces, he would have mixed emotions of relief and loss; but the emotions he did feel were not precisely those, and not mixed in the same proportions as he expected. First, England seemed unnaturally small, cramped, colourless or monochrome; the streets narrow and too loud, the cars tiny and crawling too close one to the other; the details of the people and shops and street furniture unable to be perceived with any great clarity. Second, given all that, there was actually a heatwave, so the temperature was not at all different to that in Los Angeles – it had reached a hundred and five degrees on Centre Court at Wimbledon last week, he learned – although the heat seemed to crawl closer in and make him break out into a sweat. Third, his house-mates were not all present when he arrived. Des and June were there, and greeted him warmly, and Richard, too, was around and considerably more cheerful than he had been; but Rob was said to be in the south of France teaching and would not now return, having officially left the Share household. Charlie, too had gone, to other accommodation more suited to his needs. Bode was reported to be back living permanently with his wife and kids. Phina had gone to live with her sister; and Keith and Meryl had, of course, left to get married. And then Marie.

Marie, June and Des reported, had been behaving oddly. For a few weeks, she had not attended house meetings and had stopped paying her weekly rent. Then, only a few days before K's return, she had finally announced she was leaving. Her belongings had been packed away again into bags and black rubbish sacks, and apparently one of the Greeks had taken them away in a van. And she was gone.

K went over to see John W at his office, for a debriefing about the Buttercup business. John was a little sombre. He said he had not seen Marie for a while; she had not turned up for sessions with him, and was in danger of breaching her probation order. Could K get in touch with her, and try to convey to her the gravity of this?

K had the phone number of the Greek restaurant. And eventually he got through to speak to her. She sounded unnaturally bright when she came on the line.

Are you OK? he asked.

Yes, I'm OK, she said. I'm fine. I'm working full time at the restaurant, I'm making good money.

John hasn't heard from you.

I know. Tell him I will get in touch.

You promise? He says it's serious, you have to stay in contact, otherwise you –

Yes, I know, my probation order. How was the tour?

Great. I'll tell you all about it when we meet. We will keep in contact, won't we?

Yes, of course we will. But I don't want anything more to do with the others. The rest of the household, I mean. Look, I'll call you back, only I'm on shift now.

She didn't offer any further explanation. And there the conversation ended.

K, Des and June went out to a nearby Indian restaurant, with the intention of catching up and talking about the tour. K being still in the later stages of jet-lag. But instead they mainly discussed all the departures. Des had recruited two new household members to fill the gaps: Kate, a cheerful, petite Scottish girl who had lived in one of the other short-life households but had had a bust-up with them, and a guy called Pete that K only vaguely knew, who worked for Patchwork. Meanwhile, it was definite that Sunderland Terrace would be taken back by the council within the next two months, so they would have to move.

K said he was unhappy that June and Des had taken this arbitrary decision on bringing new people into the house without consultation. What was "sharing" about, then?

Des replied reasonably that it had been necessary, otherwise the rent wouldn't be paid. K said the feedback he'd had from friends who had moved out was they felt stifled by the parental roles Des and June, and in particular Des, had assumed, and Des countered that K was only projecting this feeling onto them. But K argued that Des and June should admit what was happening, which Bode, for all his faults, had observed, should recognise the power they had in the group, rather than allow unacknowledged power struggles to destroy it, which was what had happened and was happening. And so it went on, and got rather boring.

So K, instead of feeling released from the yoke of his role over the past two or three months, found himself trapped anew in a life he was no longer choosing: exchanging one form of servitude for another. And what brought it to a head was that he heard on the grapevine that the little first-floor flat over the shop off Westbourne Grove that he had once shared with Keith, years ago, when they were fellow students, had become available again, for a rent of fifteen pounds a week, a special rate for him, the landlady, Mrs J, had told him when he'd rung her up, which was of course much more than he was currently paying into the household, but hey, if he could find a job, even if not immediately, if he could hang on for a bit longer to the money the Rock Star's empire had paid into his bank account....

And now, jet-lag notwithstanding, K, having felt all knotted up, suddenly experienced a new sort of liberation, an excitement at prospects; he could breathe again. Only the nagging worry about Marie remained in the background. As he ploughed through the accumulated correspondence that had built up in his absence, the unwellness began to dissipate. Another page could be turned, another life could begin there.

Lower Green Farm

A year or nearly as much quickly went by, and this is what ensued in that time, which was a time of plentiful optimism, before gears changed again.

K secured the rental of the flat from Mrs J within two weeks of returning from the USA, and told the household he was leaving. Des and June didn't take it very well – he was later told that June had been particularly upset – and he felt bad about that, but it was the right decision. Des offered to take his stuff over to the flat in the van; though there was some awkward quibble about K's wooden desk, which Des had actually found in a skip one day and donated to him, or shared with him, it was unclear what the nature of the transaction had been, and which K now said, to resolve the problem, he would pay for, but Des eventually demurred at that.

He needed to create some more shelving for his increasing number of books and records. He had some new planks, but not enough of the house bricks to stand them on. So when he went back to Sunderland Terrace for a last cup of tea with whoever happened to be around, he took with him the tote bag he'd bought in Beverly Hills, and before setting off again he put four or six of the bricks in it. It was ten o'clock in the evening, already dark. The Durham Castle was all lit up. As he passed, two burly white men who had been standing outside the pub suddenly crossed the road briskly towards him, shouting. They backed him up against the wall.

What have you got in that bag? demanded one.

He stuttered that it was none of their business.

Oh yes, it was. They were off-duty policemen, the bigger burly one said. Neither produced any ID to confirm that.

K had put the bag down on the pavement. He invited them to look. The second one had a small torch. Bricks. What are you doing with these? K explained in his best middle-class voice that they were intended for supporting planks to be used as bookshelves. And where did you get them from? K indicated the house behind him that had been his home. Said they were left over from building works. The men, on whose breath he smelt beer, started to lose interest. They made it clear, however, he would not be welcomed back into the neighbourhood. Then they let him go and went back inside the pub.

That was the last he saw of Sunderland Terrace. A couple of weeks later the other members of the household also had to move out, not to the promised permanent home in Kingston upon Thames, which wasn't yet ready, but to another short-life house in the neighbourhood, where they would remain for a year or so. Over the next year, he would visit there regularly to keep in contact.

Mrs J claimed to have spent two hundred pounds on refurbishing the first-floor flat, but K thought it looked exactly as it had done eight years previously when he'd shared it as a student with Keith. The grey threadbare carpet. The two single divan beds in the living/bedroom area, which he repurposed as settees, having brought over his double mattress. The net curtains. The gas heater. The heavy wardrobe. The chunky dark polished wooden table in the gloomy dining area, partitioned off from the kitchenette by frosted glass. The fridge that ran on gas: the pilot light was underneath it, so if it went out (the clue was a faint odour of gas) you had to lie on the floor and feed a lighted match through to the outlet. The payphone on the landing outside that served both this flat and the one above it, as well as the shop on the ground floor. The gloomy, tiny bathroom and solitary toilet on the ground floor, with its erratic Ascot water heater, likewise serving both flats and the shop.

K thought it was heaven. It was his.

That shop, run by Mrs J. It was a Catholic shop. It sold Catholic nick-nacks. Crucifixes in all sizes, at all levels of goriness. Rosaries: from cheap plastic ones to the really fancy rosewood and silver. Plastic statuettes of the Virgin Mary that lit up. Bibles and prayer books. Small flasks of holy water. Holy pictures of saints. Postcards depicting the current Pope. It was closed quite a lot of the time. Mrs J wasn't always in, and the eccentric fellow he remembered she used to employ to front the establishment, who wore a black, wide-brimmed hat and a cape, rode a rusty bicycle, and talked of visions of the Blessed Virgin to whomever would listen, must have gone to meet his maker years ago. And the other flat, upstairs from his own, was currently empty. When Keith and K lived there it had been occupied by a mild-mannered young Irishman called Ray who would come in from his office job every evening and then pound vigorously on an old upright piano he had up there, every single evening, making the ceiling shudder, right until lights out; when once they were invited upstairs for a cup of tea they noticed that the piano had seen its best days, and that Ray had the remains of other pianos stacked around his flat, to be cannibalised for spare parts when necessary. One day, they had heard him talking excitedly on the payphone on the landing outside, then having put the phone down he had knocked on their door to tell them the great news that he had been signed up by Tom Jones' manager, and a week later was gone, and they didn't see him again until he appeared on *Top of the Pops* under his new name, Gilbert O'Sullivan.

But what heaven, indeed. He could do whatever he liked. He wasn't lonely; he could still see his friends. On his birthday, he entertained his parents and sister, cooking them a meal in that narrow kitchenette. He rented a black-and-white portable TV. There was no room for the Roneo duplicator in the flat, but he found he could park it in the dingy basement below the shop. He discovered round the corner, on Westbourne Grove, what was billed as the only all-night supermarket in London. At two in the morning he could nip round there for a pint of milk and some frozen orange juice, maybe a bag of peanuts if he had the late-night munchies: reliving the seductive myth of total availability he had first glimpsed in the USA.

Later he re-explored the neighbourhood, so familiar from his student days. Needham Road, Artesian Road, Chepstow Villas. How they had transformed into Arcadia when he was on that memorable, if not wishing quite so much to be remembered, acid trip all those years before with Keith's friends from Halifax; those very streets actively snaking in many and wondrous colours into infinity. How the familiar old homeless guy in the ragged robes, who regularly begged a few pennies in the streets round about, made an appearance at the climax of the trip, his robes become radiant, leaving serial images of himself behind as he trudged along the road, different selves at every memory stage, psychedelic Muybridge images, photographic residues that faded only gradually; and the pale moon likewise multiplying as it rode the early evening sky towards the horizon. And the dizzying vortex that opened up therefrom, where the talking dead were, the vortex made out of the nothing he knew is all that is.

Well, he didn't really want to go back there, and these phenomena were not to be seen now, for the streets were placid and behaving themselves, solid, not snaking about out of control – but it was all good.

And he had a job. He'd seen it advertised in *Time Out*. Just down the road, eight minutes on his bicycle. Teaching Business English to foreign business people and business students. The job interview hadn't lasted long. The proprietor of the language school had been very easy-going. Enquired about his qualifications: English degree, PGCE, good. Most recent job as a private tutor: excellent. Never taught English as a foreign language before: well, never mind. Now, how would you explain to a foreign student the difference between "much" and "many" in English? he'd asked. K had blustered his way round a tortuous explanation, realising part way through that he didn't actually know the answer, but the man had interrupted him saying: Yes, that's right, "many" refers to countable quantities and "much" to uncountables. That's what he had been trying to say, claimed K. Of course, said the man. Now, when can you start? The rate was two pounds an hour, twenty hours a week to begin with, was that all right?

He didn't know the first thing about Business English, but there were textbooks provided, with useful conversational exercises.

His first student, one-to-one, was a forbidding-looking Austrian businessman who owned a company making bathroom fittings. He would fret over the inconsistencies of the English language. When K explained an anomaly of spelling or grammar he would frown and say "but zat is not logical", and K had to try to assure him that English wasn't logical at all, but that was perfectly all right. The Austrian was never convinced.

By contrast, he taught a class of young Mexican students who were in London for the summer and were boisterous and engaging. They couldn't give a fuck about what was logical or not. Wimbledon fortnight had just ended, so K conducted a conversation about that, and mentioned that he himself liked playing tennis occasionally, and they all told him simultaneously and excitedly that he should play with Miguel – they pointed to him, one of their number, a quiet lad – "He play tennis, sir!" Miguel agreed to meet at a local public tennis court in the park the following Saturday, so K dug out his old wooden tennis racket and a bunch of balls, and half the class tagged along to watch. They patted the ball to each other for a bit, and then it was agreed Miguel would serve first. Whump. The ball zinged over the net, skidded on the ground about half an inch within the service court and had disappeared behind K before he even realised it had started its trajectory. This guy was *good*. In fact, vastly too good. Out of pity, Miguel began serving at half-speed, but still took the first set six-love, and then they called it a day because it was a bit pointless. Or rather, it was K who was pointless. Well done, sir! cried the students encouragingly. Miguel shyly revealed that he was in fact the junior champion of Yucatan province in Mexico and had wanted to enter Junior Wimbledon that year, but his parents had dissuaded him, thinking it was better for his future prospects that he should come to London to study Business English.

Another one-to-one student was a young man from Senegal, an army officer who revealed that he worked as a bodyguard for the President of his country, and had been sent to London for a few weeks to improve his English. He would stand to attention and click his heels when K entered the room, despite being repeatedly assured that this was not necessary. The lessons would consist of amiable conversations about life in England. This Senegalese bodyguard called K by his surname, under the evident impression that this was what was required – he said he was fond of reading stories about English public school life – and he complimented K warmly on his "Oxford accent".

It was the hottest summer in living memory. He went to Hyde Park with some friends, and they swam in the Serpentine. Keith and Meryl visited London with their newly acquired red setter, a lively dog, and called in to see him; Keith was amused at K's winding up back in the old flat. He was working for a fringe theatre company in Halifax. Meryl was looking very well.

There was no more news on the Marie front; John W said he was trying to re-establish regular contact with her. In passing, he assured K the head teacher of Buttercup's school had been satisfied he had done his best, under the circumstances.

K was surprised to find that he grew to dislike talking about the US tour. Whenever he was round at the old Share house, or rather, the new old house, someone would invariably bring up the topic and urge him to tell the tale again to someone else who hadn't heard it before. At first, he enjoyed this attention. But he became, first, bored, then disillusioned. For the attention being paid was invariably not to the essence he perceived in the tale, the nugget hidden within it, which he was forever trying to bring out, and make better sense of, but to what he regarded as superficial features the listeners were fascinated by, and which he regarded as unimportant – and that created bad faith. Yet he found he was developing a way of telling it, a routine, which began to disgust him if that's not too strong a way of putting it. There were, for example, many different ways of answering the question "But what was he *really* like?" – none of them satisfactory or authentic, yet he felt obliged to try them out. And soon he began to despise that, and also to despise himself for his compliance, but he didn't really enjoy despising. Once, at a dinner party he had been invited to in North London by some old friends, the topic had predictably arisen – "Oh, K, do tell us about that, listen everybody, this is incredible" – and a very attractive woman who had been full of herself all evening and had up till then paid him no attention whatsoever suddenly began to dote on his every word and to give every evidence of finding him utterly fascinating, to the extent that he started to regard this woman, who had initially seemed alluring and tantalisingly out of reach of his desire, with increasing contempt. There was, admittedly, a measure of self-regard in this contempt; he desperately wanted to be valued, as anyone does, for what he felt was of absolute value within himself, an integral creativity, let us say; and it was therefore disappointing to find himself becoming a mere object of exchange value in a system he hadn't wanted to subscribe to in the first place.

The writing continued. He was developing his short stories as well as the poems. Two stories had been published in that prestigious Anglo-American magazine, and now a third, his best yet he thought, had been accepted for an annual Arts Council-sponsored anthology of stories by new writers.

At a five-day residential writing course run by the Arvon Foundation in Devon he met a new friend, Jonathan, who was an aspiring novelist. The course was run by Emma Tennant and Elaine Feinstein. Emma Tennant, who was an imposing and handsome woman of a certain age, with an air of great enthusiasm and bountifulness, was starting a high-profile magazine of new writing called *Bananas*. She was very enthusiastic about K's short fiction, comparing him favourably – because he "cared about his characters" – to the young Turk Martin Amis (whose first novel had recently been published, and whom K had not read). There were around a dozen students on the course. Angela Carter was the visiting reader at the weekend. The climax of the proceedings was meant to be a visitation by Ted Hughes, who owned the house where these courses took place; he had in tow no less a personage than Yevgeny Yevtushenko, the famous Russian poet. Yevtushenko was very flamboyantly Russian, kissing all the women who were present and making extravagant statements in every direction. Most of the students were in awe, but Jonathan and K bunked off while the readings and speeches were taking place, and found Angela Carter, who had also escaped the shenanigans, sitting on the floor on her own by the fire. They spent an hour or two talking with Angela Carter, who was kittenishly playful with a good helping of cynical wit, and was a great antidote to the literary pompousness going on in the next room. They didn't talk writing much but laughed uproariously and repeatedly. Eventually Yevtushenko and Ted Hughes went away.

And after that, K kept in contact with Jonathan, who was an interesting writer and had interesting contacts, really quite separate from the poetry scene he was starting to know so well now, and Emma Tennant also kept in touch and asked him for a piece for *Bananas*. So he sent a new story, and it was published. Then another one. And that previous one was also published, the one in that Arts Council anthology, and he went to the launch party, and was feted, and the fiction editor of *Woman's Own* asked him as a matter of fact how much had he been paid for that story, and he answered proudly "Ninety pounds" (the most he'd ever earned from writing in his short writing life), and she said scornfully was that all? he could earn much more writing genre fiction for *Woman's Own*, he should try it, so he said he'd think about that. And an editor from Chatto & Windus or was it Faber congratulated him on his story and said he'd really like to see a novel from him – they were scooping up the young writers then – but K didn't like to admit he had no idea how to develop his shtick to novel length, and also he had a feeling this editor would subtly push him in a direction he didn't want to go but would not have the confidence to resist. He thought he would pick Jonathan's brains, for Jonathan had, amazingly, already completed two novels. And an excerpt from one of them was to be published in *Vogue*. And Jonathan had told K that Hutchinson or was it Allison & Busby might be interested in publishing one or both in their entirety, which awed him immensely. As for K, was he a poet or a novelist? Jonathan observed that when he read his prose aloud he conducted the rhythms of his own sentences with his right hand as the narrative proceeded or didn't proceed – for what that was worth.

Phew.

A poetry reading in a gallery in Hammersmith. It was organised by a strange character called Cory Harding, who much later fell out with most of the poets he had promoted. Robert was there, also Mike Dobbie. Paul Green, the editor of *Spectacular Diseases* magazine, had been billed to appear, but no-one had ever seen him, so when the time came Cory Harding called out "Now Paul Green – is Paul Green here?" And a long-haired, long-bearded man in a donkey jacket shuffled forward from the back, a sheaf of papers in his hands. When he got to the front, he immediately started reading from his sheaf, in a low, inaudible mumble. Someone at the back said politely "Could you speak up a bit?" but Paul Green, if indeed it was he, took no notice but continued the low-profile delivery. When he had finished, he shuffled back to the back of the room without a further word of any kind.

When it came to *his* turn to read, K did not read his own work but instead the whole of Gertrude Stein's "Before the flowers of friendship faded, friendship faded", which had been obsessing him for a while.

Robert and Mike and K went to Eric Mottram's house in Herne Hill, where they spent the entire evening. The house was a labyrinth of books, piles of sheet music, LP records, prints in and out of frames. Brooding over everything from a high corner, unmentionable things spilled out of a battered old suitcase: a sculpture by Jeff Nuttall. On the piano, some music by Webern. But Eric Mottram, who talked himself hoarse, was too shy to play anything in front of them. He talked instead about Americans' obsession with guns and motor cars, about which he knew a great deal, and about contemporary poetry, about which he knew practically everything anyone could know. They drank red wine. Mike explained his plan to publish a series of twelve broadsheets, each featuring a poem by a single poet, together with their passport photo, the set to be called "Mugshots". All those present were invited to contribute. Towards the end of the evening Mike, a racing buff, tipped The Minstrel, with Lester Piggott up, for next day's Derby. The following morning, K, with a bit of a hangover, went over to the bookie's opposite his flat and put 50p on it, and it came in first by a neck.

With Robert, Mike and Ulli McCarthy (soon to be Freer) he put on a series of readings at the White Swan pub in Covent Garden. The series was called "Future Events". By now, the Poetry Society in Earl's Court was no longer the place to be, The Man having re-taken control, and the Interesting Poets, having put up rather feeble resistance, had retreated. Among the poets scheduled at the White Swan, then, was one K had published a pamphlet by, Paul St Vincent, whose work had arrived unsolicited but had stood out from the dross – but he had never actually met him. So when this black guy turned up apologising that Paul St Vincent couldn't make it, and offering to read Paul St Vincent's poems himself, K agreed; and this Paul St Vincent impersonator did it very well, and it was not till later that the penny dropped and he realised that E A "Archie" Markham, for this was the charming young man who had turned up, and Paul St Vincent were one and the same person housing two distinct poets.

K met up with Des and June again. Des was still regularly going up to the Roundhouse in Chalk Farm, as he had been doing for a year or two. He had a stall there selling button badges at gigs. That was one of his many businesses: he had invested in a second-hand badge-making machine which enabled anyone to make a badge to their own specifications and design. Now the Roundhouse gigs were still going strong, and also the badge business, but there was a change in the air, Des said. K remembered going to the Roundhouse to see the likes of Hawkwind, the Edgar Broughton Band, and the hippie commune band Quintessence, who journeyed through hour-long, ecstatic modal improvisations, fuelled by cannabis, acid, incense and mind-bending strobe lighting. But that was all long gone now, said Des. The kids were into a different kind of music now, much faster and more high-energy. The drugs were different too. He was going up there again next weekend to set up his badge stall, the headliners being a new band called The Clash. They were hysterically popular with the kids. (Both of them had now fallen unconsciously into calling the audience "the kids".) The bands all had aggressive names like that now, The Damned, Crass, The Stranglers; the hippie days were definitely over.

June mentioned that she and Des were going to see Bode, did K want to come? He was all right now, she hastily added. He was living quietly with Elsa and the children in West Mersea in Essex. They were going to have an encounter weekend. Bode was running encounter groups for a living now. To his own surprise, K agreed to come along. And he did, and found Bode apparently at peace with himself and his family. The four of them – Bode, Des, June and K – had five two-hour sessions of gentle living theatre over the weekend in a bare room in the house Bode and Elsa were renting near the beach, which Bode was advertising as the Process Centre. K found it very interesting. For example, the following exchange:

June told the little group her problem was she took out her anger with others on herself.

Bode: When you say that you take out your anger with others on yourself, who would be the main person to arouse these feelings?

June (smiling): Who do you think. (Pause.) Des, of course.

Bode: And who behind Des?

June: A nest full of eggs.

Then the session meandered to a close. And at the next, Bode said he had made a mistake. As soon as June said "A nest full of eggs", he should have said "*mu*" or "photograph", and ended it there. Because nothing more needed to be said.

K: But that doesn't get us anywhere!

Bode: (Put his forefinger up, and smiled enigmatically.) *Mu*.

Later, they all went down to the beach with the children. Bode told K a long story about a doppelganger, which he gave permission for K to use in his work. K showed one of his poems, which he called "The Circulation of the Light"

> there is wizardry
> in what manner & by what processes
> stars become dust

and Bode responded with great enthusiasm, saying that that was what he meant, that the way the poem had been composed, three lines that had grouped themselves by chance, or chance-enhanced decision, showed its own Process. And there was nothing further to say, because the poem *was* its own saying.

Coming back to London, K felt a great sadness about everything that had been found and lost, come to light come to dust and the rest of it. He decided he couldn't write another poem. But then his friend Robert, with whom he on-and-off edited *Alembic* poetry magazine, whose next issue was perennially imminent, rang to say did he know visiting American poets Robert Creeley and Fielding Dawson were reading at the Air Gallery. He took the call on the payphone in the hallway. So he said yes, he'd meet Robert there, and they could have a chat about the magazine.

He arrived late, people were drifting in to the performance area of the gallery, and it was time for the reading to begin. Wine was being served, but it was expensive. There was Robert. The space was crowded – the audience sat on plastic chairs in concentric semi-circles. There were no vacant chairs, therefore they sat on the floor. They saw their mutual friend David Miller, the Australian poet, who lived near K, off Ladbroke Grove, and who would also be in the next issue of their magazine – he had managed to secure a seat. White lights shone. American voices could be heard. The readers were allocated chairs, a low table with a pitcher of water and glasses, a microphone. To the readers' right, there was a large grey-brown-white abstract impressionist style painting, to their left a set of brightly coloured geometrical abstracts, and behind them some energetic semi-representational pictures done in gouache or some such medium.

Both Robert Creeley and Fielding Dawson could be seen talking with the organisers and also with a man Robert identified as Robert Duncan, another celebrated American poet, who was visiting Britain but not reading tonight. Both readers kept their coats on, even though it was warm under the gallery lights. Fielding Dawson was actually sweating – you could see a thin shiny line of perspiration running down the left side of his face. And Robert Creeley kept his hat on. It was a kind of bush hat with little ventilating holes, and his coat was army olive drab with a sort of fur collar. He had only one functioning eye. Fielding Dawson wore an old raincoat and jeans.

They were both asked questions. Then Fielding Dawson read first, followed by Robert Creeley. From the audience, Robert Duncan made the occasional comment. When you read the books, thought K, it's literature; but when you hear it spoken it's a person – a man writing. Making choices of words, choices that might have been, that could still be, different.

Both readers smoked cigarettes throughout, even though the organising woman had made a plea to everyone not to smoke. Both seemed younger than their years, in Fielding Dawson's case boyish. Fielding Dawson spoke of drinking beer in the 1950s, Robert Creeley of getting stoned in New Zealand, where he had spent time. Maybe that was where he had acquired the bush hat. Fielding Dawson's speech was exactly like his written prose, jumping about and quite fine. Robert Creeley's final poem about his mother was, K thought, exceptionally moving. Though you weren't supposed to say "moving" in these poetry scenes, he knew; he had been gently chastised for that.

At the break, Robert and K talked about who would be in the next issue of their magazine. K had started a correspondence with James Sherry, the poet he had met by accident in Manhattan, who had promised to send some work. James' own magazine was now coming out regularly, each issue posted to K's new address from New York. Well, that was a bit like the change that was happening at the Roundhouse. Where before those pages had been filled with familiar names, those indeed of the generation of Creeley and Dawson – Allen Ginsberg, Michael McClure, Anne Waldman and the rest – the new issues had less familiar contributors: Bruce Andrews, Charles Bernstein, Ray DiPalma, Mei-Mei Berssenbrugge, and a host of others. But not only that, the work, no less than the roll-call of names, was unfamiliar; there was clearly a New New Thing happening, much of which would at first glance be incomprehensible to many of those gathered here this evening. It was like the New American Poetry was Yes, Genesis, Pink Floyd, the Moody Blues, and the New New Thing now emerging on those pages was X-Ray Spex, The Slits or The Clash.

So K and Robert agreed James would be in the upcoming issue of their magazine, because this was all interesting, and also included would be Alan Davies, a Canadian poet resident in New York who seemed to be friendly with this new crowd, and with whom K had also been corresponding. K had sent Alan Davies some recent work, and Alan Davies had critiqued it at some length but with plenty of positive vibe, questioning K's continuing adherence to Surrealism, praising specific lines that seemed to depart from what could be viewed as familiar avant-garde tropes and to head off in an opposite direction, so K thought that was very interesting and useful.

He continued to run off pages of poetry on the Roneo that was now ensconced in the dim cellar below his flat, below the shop; in between fretting that he wasn't making progress writing that damn novel. He started breaking up the novel-not-in-progress, putting its sentences and fragments of sentences and fragments of fragments into new juxtapositions, longing to find combinations that didn't actively make him feel sick.

He was contacted by someone whose name was familiar in the alternative poetry little magazine scene. A young woman poet, unusually in that scene in those days. She had heard he had a duplicator; she needed a pamphlet, a collection of her poems, to be run off. It turned out she lived only a couple of streets away, in the direction of Portobello Road and Ladbroke Grove. So she came round to the flat. She was slim, fair-haired, slanting grey eyes, very attractive, and she had a toddler in tow. She showed some of her poems to K; they were all right. Not great, but all right. He promised to help her. She invited him round to where she was living for a cup of tea; it was a squat she shared with her boyfriend, who was not present – he was a working musician, apparently. There were gig posters on the walls, and the toddler played happily with his toys on the floor. On the next occasion that she called round to K's, to collect the run-off sheets, she was unencumbered by the child. He was being looked after, she explained. It was late in the evening. All of a sudden, she moved closer to him and demanded that he kiss her; which, startled, he did. Then she offered her person to him shyly. That is to say, she slowly removed most of her clothing. And then they did the deed on K's mattress in a rather fumbling way. So that was very welcome, but it confused things no end. K had not heard from Marie in ever such a long while, and, well, it had been a frustrating time. So then, they did it on at least one more occasion, but then when they met for a final time at a poetry reading at Pentameters one wet October night she said they could not continue, and K felt mingled distress and relief. He never met the boyfriend, thankfully. All that was left was the memory of her patchouli scent, and some rejected pages from the duplicator. He was not to know that thirty or so years later he would write a freely extemporised version of her into a novel, the novel he could not possibly have written at the time.

Instead, he continued to break up and redistribute his own previous writings, often working to a background of blues and jazz, reggae and improvised music spinning on his turntable, working into the night in the flat, sometimes after the pub opposite had shut its doors officially and was having a lively if muffled lock-in. This was poetry of a new sort, jagged yet the jags free-flowing, at least that was the effect he imagined and hoped for. He went in to the Business English school and put in some more teaching hours to pay the rent, though the hours were starting to dwindle as the season faded. He wandered up and down Portobello Road to do his shopping or mooch among second-hand record stalls and shops, came back, plunged frantically into writing: about fruit, fakes, clothes and classical terraces in decline, about Rasta men in the communal gardens, elderly ladies poking vegetables offered for sale; about sitar players under the flyover, and about the outrageous grandeur of fortunes that presented in inside-out fashion. How wild it all was. That sort of thing, it all went in, the language of description savagely cut, pasted, cut again, spliced into new contexts. There was despair in it at the impossibility of a narrative, but joy too that anything else might be possible. Well, he was amassing a book of this stuff. And that would be the first one to be published, within the next three or four years (after bits had found their way one by one into various magazines), not by his own or Mike's imprint, but by a major small press, one of the cooler ones of that era, though they didn't use words like cool at that time.

The days went by so fast, time seemed almost made of liquid.

That was how almost a year passed.

•

It all came to a halt quite suddenly, as July turned into August again. K had had a good June and July. Through his sister, he had met Lynne. She was going to be the next great love of his life. Lovely girl. Architecture student, very artistic. Involved with the Chile Solidarity Campaign. His sister's second-husband-to-be had suggested the four of them hire a camper van and travel around Europe but that never happened. Lynne and K had spent a wonderful weekend in his flat, wandered around a local street fair where Tom Baker, guesting in his Dr Who role, was also wandering morosely, in his hat and long, multi-coloured scarf. Went to a showing of *Giant* with James Dean at the wonderfully dilapidated Electric Cinema on Portobello Road. They lingered, gave each other presents of books. Over a couple of weeks, at her digs in Clapham, K helped Lynne construct a model of the building she was designing for her final exams. It was summer, not in itself as exquisite a summer as the one before, but one that held a lot of promise.

But then officials from the Gas Board turned up one early August morning at K's flat to turn off the gas supply. They wouldn't speak, they were just following orders; but it turned out Mrs J had not paid her bill. It was unclear whether she had some dispute with the Gas Board or was simply unable to pay. The shop hadn't been doing very well; in fact, it had been closed most of the time recently. K made his feelings quite clear to Mrs J. So Mrs J provided him with an electric kettle, and also installed a calor gas stove. As it was still summer, room heating wasn't required. But he couldn't have a bath, unless he wanted a cold one. And the gas-powered fridge was, of course, out of action. He went over to his parents' flat (they were away on holiday) to use their bath and cook himself a meal.

It was not the first time he'd been at odds with Mrs J. During the winter, when Business English teaching hours had dried up and he found himself jobless and having to sign on at the SS again, she had refused to provide a rent book, which he needed in order to show the SS. The rent had always been handed over in cash each week. So K had gone to WH Smith's to purchase a rent book, in which he forged entries since the previous July, taking care to weather the book a little for verisimilitude. To his relief, it worked. In fact, he regretted he hadn't used the opportunity to inflate the rent figure a little, for some added value.

Now came the second metaphorical kick to the groin. Lynne had started being elusive. No, she couldn't meet him next weekend, maybe the weekend after? And then the fateful postcard had arrived from her telling him she was off to Spain with her friend for a month and couldn't spare the time to see him beforehand. That had all been going so promisingly. Perhaps he should have got an inkling when on a July weekend at her parents' farm in Hampshire he had been persuaded to mount a horse which seemed the size of an elephant and he had been terrified. Or when she had said she wanted "lots of children", which had probably terrified him even more. Well, anyway, there was the postcard from her, effectively dumping him while urging him not to be "alone with his grief"; to add to the letter in which she had asserted that Krishnamurti had said the followers of Zen were "doomed" (he had tried to explain to her what Zen meant to him), and by implication provided him with the assessment that his standing as a poet, even as a poet with some Hispanic blood, whatever that meant, and generally as a man of sensitivity and grace, had been found wanting.

And that was when he had unburdened himself to Henning the Dane in the Patchwork office in Ladbroke Grove, where he had gone to do a couple of days' admin work, for he badly needed the money (even though he was now withholding the rent in protest against Mrs J), because the language school hours had never quite revived this season.

And that was when Henning said: There is this beautiful house available, but it's outside London. Lower Green Farm.

If you can put together a group of people. You might want to consider that.

•

When K visited Robert two days later to talk again about the upcoming sixth issue of the poetry magazine, he mentioned the Lower Green Farm proposition.

It was now mid-August. Although this summer had not been a match for that of the year before, a typically unstable English mini-heatwave was lingering, with thunder in the air. Robert was at the time living in the latest of a succession of furnished bedsits in North London. His girlfriend Sibani wrote children's stories in Bengali. They had talked previously, idly, about founding a community of poets. Not just poets, but writers. Not just writers, but artists, musicians, film-makers. It was a fantasy, really. That was why K brought up the subject of Lower Green Farm, about which he was still highly dubious, in such a throwaway fashion.

To K's surprise, Robert was seriously interested. Robert was a tall man, calm and cautious in his demeanour, but with a twinkle in his eye from time to time. He had always been curious about K's other existence in the short-life housing world. But K did not think Robert would cope with communal living, and doubted he would follow through. It was too big a step.

•

A new development. Mrs J now made a dramatic announcement: she was selling up. That was it, she'd had enough. She had just put her property on the market with the estate agents next door, and she would have to give K notice. Which was ridiculous, because he didn't even have a proper tenancy. But legally he supposed he could assert squatter's rights and remain there, and she would have a big problem on her hands. He didn't say this exactly. He just said he had nowhere else to go, so until he did he would have to stay where he was. In response, she gave him a brochure from the same estate agents, listing details of beautiful properties in the neighbourhood he might like to investigate. What planet was she on? If, as she knew full well, he didn't even have a proper job, how could he contemplate buying a property? If he had the means to buy a property, why would he be living in that crummy flat for fifteen pounds a week?

•

So Vicky, the Patchwork Housing Association administrator, offered to drive K to see Lower Green Farm, and Robert, on being asked, agreed to come along. Neither K nor Robert could drive – they were poets, after all. It was warm and humid. The radio in Nicky's car predicted "severe weather in the Greater London area". The previous night, a consultation of the I Ching had resulted in the advice to K to proceed with restraint: "A marriage entered into now would not last long." So that was a warning.

They drove out of London, across the river and on into the south-eastern suburbs, the names getting weirder. Bromley, Orpington, Green Street Green, and beyond that Pratt's Bottom.

The joke about Pratt's Bottom was left unmentioned because, as it happened, Vicky's surname was Pratt. So it was a dwarf elephant in that little room that was her car. She was a nice young woman. She listened intently to K as he outlined what now seemed to be the Project. They made slow progress, all the traffic lights were against them. The Project, K explained, the Project as he was calling it, it did seem to have acquired a capital P, was about putting together an artistic community of poets, writers, artists, musicians, film-makers, whatever, who were outside the mainstream. She nodded and smiled. Robert interjected from time to time.

They reached Lower Green Farm about lunchtime. There was some discussion about why it had that name. It was approached by an unmade road off the main road to Sevenoaks, horribly bumpy. The garden surrounding it was huge and densely overgrown. Vicky parked the car in the road outside, half on a verge, and they walked through the wide main gateway and into the grounds. There were two outhouses, right and left, either side of the front path. Winding paths branched off the main path and disappeared along the sides of the house, leading to the back. There was fancy brickwork, fringed with weeds. There were ruined archways.

The front door was painted a blue that had faded, and nestled in a portico fronted with columns. The house looked neither like a suburban home nor an English farmhouse. Italianate was a word Robert introduced to the conversation. Vicky had the key.

An entrance lobby gave onto the room that would have been the kitchen. There was a large boiler in a chimney-breast area. Vicky said she had been told it was still capable of being fired up. It was oil-fired: the oil would come through a pipe from a side-annexe where the storage tank was, and the boiler would drive the central heating system. No furniture anywhere. The ground floor also contained two large rooms with many-paned windows giving onto the side of the house that faced dense undergrowth, and whereas the kitchen was plain, its walls painted cream, with rough, bare floorboards, these rooms had richly gleaming parquet flooring, wood-panelling on all walls and those long crystalline windows. There was tranquillity here. They could hear the fourfold warble of a wood pigeon outside, and beyond that, a faint hum of traffic.

Upstairs, off a long corridor, there were five possible bedrooms of various sizes, and a bathroom.

They looked around extensively. It all appeared to be in reasonably good order. The house seemed a long way from the centre of things. But it was a haven. It was indeed beautiful.

Vicky told K and Robert as she was closing the front door behind them that if they were interested they needed to discuss the details with Henning and Bruce in the Patchwork office.

K felt the necessity of buying Vicky a drink. Once she'd locked up, they ventured out onto the main road and found a quiet suburban pub a little way off. Vicky said she would have an orange juice and lemonade, as she was driving. Robert asked for a pint, and K opted for a half of bitter. The publican served the half in a stemmed glass. When he realised this was for K, not "the lady", he became distraught, imploring forgiveness, fearing he'd impugned K's manhood by not using a straight glass or a mug. It was as much as K could do to assure him it really didn't matter. He carried the drinks to the table where Vicky and Robert had settled, and told them about this. They laughed.

We're not in London any more, said Robert solemnly, Dorothy-like, and they all laughed some more.

On their return to the capital, as the rain started to arrive, reports were coming over Vicky's car radio that Elvis Presley had died suddenly, aged 42.

•

So this was now a Project. Who might be interested in joining them? They needed to put together a group of at least half a dozen to make it financially viable. Robert, Sibani, K – that was three. Who else? Possibly David Miller, known to be unhappy in his digs in Notting Hill, where he often complained of the noise. That was three poets and a children's story writer. What about Allen Fisher, who was both a poet and a painter? But Allen was perfectly OK where he was in South London. Robert asked about their former mutual college mate Keith, but K said he had just married Meryl, and they had moved back up north where they had family. Jonathan, K's novelist friend? Maybe. Perhaps some women to even things up.

•

K cycled to Islington, where Jonathan was squatting with his ex-Cambridge punk friends. He'd been asked to return the manuscript of the latest of Jonathan's novels that he had been reading – Jonathan needed it back, because Allison & Busby had lost his only other copy.

The flat was over a drinking club in a part of Islington that was being torn apart in the continuing process of gentrification, and it was accessed via an outdoor iron staircase. One of Jonathan's punk friends played in a band that was getting quite popular. Their single had reached number 42 in the national charts. Jonathan was working as a barman, he said. His attractive girlfriend was helping him paint the flat while waiting to buy her own house. She had money of her own.

When K arrived, Jonathan immediately put a single on the turntable – namesake Jonathan Richman & the Modern Lovers – and started to roll a joint on a nearby LP cover. Listen to this, he said, it's great. He disapproved of K's recent penchant for Little Feat. It was all about the New Wave now, he said. Singles printed on coloured vinyl, with photocopied sleeves. Yes, Jonathan was in love with the modern world.

They reminisced, as they ate biscuits and drank coffee, about how at that party at Emma Tennant's London town house, attended by Harold Pinter and Lady Antonia Fraser, where they were guests as contributors to *Bananas*, they had met and talked for an hour with an increasingly inebriated and jovial J G Ballard, who was disinclined to join the great and the good visible at the other end of the vast living room and perfectly happy to talk to them for the duration of the evening, rather as Angela Carter had been. At the conversation's height, Ballard, now sailing merrily on the high seas of discourse, had pointed up at the overhead light fitting and announced: "McLuhan says a light bulb is pure information", breaking into copious giggles at that point.

Jonathan said, jokingly – although he meant it – that he had been embarrassed when K, also by now somewhat flushed following several glasses of white wine, had shouted to Jim Ballard as they were leaving "I love your work!" K said he didn't regret saying this, but he thought Ballard had not heard it anyway.

They talked again about K's adventure in the States the previous year with the Rock Star. The conversation meandered pleasantly, fuelled admirably by the joint they had consumed. But the upshot was Jonathan was not interested in moving out of London.

Nor did K himself really want to either. But there didn't seem any other viable options. Now at the tail end of August the Notting Hill Carnival came around, and K met some friends from the Share household on the Sunday, also Rob, who was of course no longer with the household but living nearby with his girlfriend, and then again on Monday for the start of the procession. It was great to be out on the streets. Incense, frying food, people telling each other to "take care", a ten-year-old kid playing drums in virtuoso fashion. A buzzy helicopter in the blue sky. White sun. Insects bit.

On Monday evening, Robert and Sibani and David Miller arrived at K's flat to talk about plans for the Lower Green Farm Project, as it now was. So there were four of them. David said he had been avoiding the Carnival. He hated it. He had stayed indoors all weekend, only venturing out for this meeting. But he mentioned his painter friend Norman, newly arrived from Australia and kipping on his floor, was looking for a home and might also be interested in the Project. Could be a fifth member. It looked good anyway.

At that point, there was an intense commotion outside in the dusk. Sirens and screaming. They tried to peer out of the kitchenette window at the back of the flat. A black youth had got into the back yard, pursued by two cops. He was clearly very frightened, whimpering like a cornered animal. The policemen and their accompanying shadows jumped over the fence after him; they were shouting, something about a knife. That poor young guy was fucked, it seemed to them watching: there was no possibility of his arguing, Actually, officers, this knife is one I use solely to sharpen my pencils, which are for personal use in my work as an artist and poet. And there was no way the police would then say, Oh, sorry sir, apologies for troubling you, we do agree there is no evidence to suggest otherwise, so a good evening to you and we'll be on our way. No, they smothered him on the ground, thuggishly, then hauled him back over the fence and dragged him to the waiting police vehicle, which couldn't quite be seen, only its pulsing blue light reflected on the pavement.

•

Henning was driving. Bruce, another manager from the Patchwork Housing Association, was with him, and K was in the back seat. Hot September day. Bruce, dark, hairy and bearded, said he was uptight because his lady was leaving him. K said he'd been there. And quite recently. Henning was his usual chilled-out peaceful Viking self. Bruce insisted on playing his tape of The Eagles on the car stereo for the entirety of the journey – always a bad sign. K wondered if he could stand it the third time "Hotel California" came round.

They parked at Green Street Green before arriving at the house, and Henning announced they were going to have lunch on Patchwork expenses. The restaurant was would-be swanky, with French on the menu and bad prints on the orange walls. Drinks before, during and after a somewhat indifferent meal: K found the veal was chewy, the vegetables distinctly unexciting. Henning observed that five years ago the likes of them, with the way they looked, would not have been allowed on these premises.

When they reached Lower Green Farm, they found there had been a break-in. But relax, it's not serious, said Henning calmly. Probably local kids. The stuff that had been left in the house on a previous Patchwork workforce visit was all still there, bar a couple of boxes of matches. A corner of the ceiling in one of the smaller upstairs bedrooms had fallen in. Ah, two slates missing from the roof there, said Henning, having nipped outside for a look. He promised the Patchwork workforce would get all problems sorted and all work done within three days. The electricity was working, the water not (Henning said he would contact the Water Board). The central heating looked new, but wasn't working either; they'd get someone in to look at it. All work to be costed and paid for in kind; that was to say, there would be a deduction from the rent. Outlay on all materials to be refunded. So it was going forward.

•

A thin line of smoke, barely a thread, stands vertically still, poised on the tip of the joss-stick in its little brass holder on the bottom bookshelf. At the next shelf up its stillness begins to be interrupted; perturbations gradually intervene, it starts to curl in complicated ways and then to flatten itself in front of the books stored there, crawling upward against and caressing their spines before breaking up, losing coherence in a hazy pall gradually thinning to nothingness at the third shelf. It looks as though the books are starting to catch fire.

K was alone with the silence that followed the final track of the Beach Boys' *Surf's Up*, most of his possessions surrounding him, the books back on their shelves, the voided boxes littering the floor, but nobody else yet inhabiting the house. During the day, sunshine poured through the foliage and double glazing. As evening came on, he could see stars outside.

Nobody else in that big house.

He hadn't been the first inhabitant. That had been Norman. David Miller had changed his mind at the last minute and declined to join the Project, but his friend Norman, who had nowhere else to lay his head but on the floor in David's digs, had volunteered to go on ahead. He said he would camp out with his sleeping bag in one of the upper bedrooms and look after the place for a few days. Only it hadn't worked out. Spooked by the isolation after two days and nights, despite a flying visit by K bringing him an electric heater – because the nights were suddenly growing cold and the central heating still wasn't on – he had finally escaped back to London, then, depressed, had according to reports gone on a binge in Soho, spending £25, all the cash he had on him, on a "relief massage" and losing his pullover in the process. So that was the end of that.

It had been a dizzying week. K travelled down with the Patchwork workforce, who spent three days working at the house. He had spent one night in his sleeping bag there before going back to London with Henning in the Godfrey Davis van; waiting for Des and his van to become available to transport his things. Robert paid a visit in advance of his furniture arriving, to inspect the place. He had been promised a whole houseful of it, gratis, by a friend, he said. Robert was exceedingly nervous of the prowling kids, who had been deemed harmless by Henning – who assured him they'd had plenty of time to vandalise the place and hadn't done so, ergo they weren't going to. They were suburban middle-class kids. K went back to London to catch a poetry reading at the Enterprise in Chalk Farm with the usual crowd: David Miller, Paul Brown, Bernard Kelly and Philip Jenkins, who was a very good poet and amusing prose writer that David knew. Bernard Kelly was in good form but his Dadaist friends were being unpleasant. K missed David's performance on clarinet; he just caught him leaving with his drummer, who had had an argument with Kelly.

The following weekend Des transported furniture gathered from Robert's friends and also from K's sister. Things were not right: a mains fuse had blown twice, the telephone had been installed but didn't work, K's Roneo duplicator had been broken in transit, the central heating engineer had not kept his appointment, and the Patchwork workforce had suddenly departed, leaving the bedroom ceiling job half done. It was now October. It was getting cold, the central heating was still inoperable, and there was no prospect of any other residents for the Project. K returned to London yet again to have a bath and a meal at his parents', then on to see Des and June and his other friends at the Share household, where he spent the night in a sleeping bag amid the smell of cats, with the electric bar firelight bouncing off dusty Melanex wallpaper. He was still having to sign on at the SS in Bayswater every fortnight. He visited Bob Cobbing in the morning to get some stencils cut for *Alembic* magazine; the Scottish poet Tom Leonard was there, because Cobbing was publishing a booklet of his, and they were all pretty jolly. He met up with Rhoda again, visiting from New York with her boyfriend, the contemporary classical percussionist Richard, who had a gig at the Wigmore Hall.

But the phone was now at last working at Lower Green Farm, and who should ring out of the blue but Marie.

It was just like old times. She was so chatty. She and K spoke for an immensely long time. K took the call in the panelled living room, watching spiders weaving their delicate sun-outlined webs outside the window as they talked. Marie said she was well. She was now a trainee manager with the Pizzaland chain of restaurants, with plenty of prospects, and was back living in Westbourne Park Road, in the same building as ex-Share household member Rob, and also where John W now had his office. She was sharing a room there. She promised to visit K. And on her day off, so she did. She joined Robert and K for an evening meal in Lower Green Farm which K cooked, and afterwards they played Monopoly and she bankrupted them both. She loved the house. Robert and K wondered if she wanted to join them. If she lived there, she said she might try to get a transfer to the Pizzaland branch in Croydon; she could commute on the train from Orpington to East Croydon then. That was a plan, anyway. By then, it was too late for her to get back to London, so K offered her his bed and she invited him in. But she made no sexual overtures, and so they slept chastely together that night.

•

So Robert and K, having run out of ideas about other potential residents who might contribute to the artistic life of the incipient community, were obliged to advertise in *Time Out*, in the "Rooms offered" section. (Robert's partner, Sibani, had also effectively bowed out of the Project because by now she was teaching full-time in Bedford and could only come down for weekends, so they were down to two, plus Marie.)

At first, this plan didn't seem very promising. Despite the

plea in the advert for writers, poets, artists, photographers to join an artistic community, most respondents were just looking for a cheap place to live.

But among those first applicants were a couple who sounded more like it. They arrived for interview in an ancient Citroen. They were Erik, a big man of Norwegian-American origin with piercing blue eyes and a substantial black beard (he later told K he had never shaved in his life) and his German wife Almut, who seemed warm and friendly. They had been living in Berlin, or West Berlin as it then was, for some years, though he hailed originally from Detroit and she from Frankfurt. They, Robert and K immediately took to each other. Amazingly, they had English poet friends in common: Allen Fisher (Erik worked at the War on Want print shop in London with Allen's Aloes Books associate, Jim Pennington), Cris Cheek, Lawrence Upton, Ulli McCarthy (not yet Freer).

The couple fitted in very well, and Erik turned out to be a significant artistic presence at Lower Green Farm.

Erik went under the name E E Vonna-Michell for the purpose of his artistic activities. The E E stood for Erik Edward – though he introduced himself as Erik, his wife, confusingly, called him Ed, and he called her by the nickname Muthis, which everybody adopted.

His work as an artist was very much in what some might have termed the neo-Dada or post-Duchamp area, though he mischievously disavowed all antecedents. However, he was an admirer of the Swiss artist Dieter Roth, in particular those book works that questioned the very identity of the book and the notion of readability, and also those pieces made from organic matter, exhibiting a fascination for the processes of decay. While at Lower Green Farm, and previously and afterwards, he made works in a variety of media, usually under the imprint Balsam Flex. He put out a series of lo-fi cassettes of noise pieces, including one by the sound-poet Henri Chopin, one in which he interviewed Allen Fisher in an automated car wash (the conversation almost entirely swamped by car wash sounds) and various sound-text performances by Cris Cheek and Lawrence Upton, who were to be regular visitors at Lower Green Farm. He made objects that defied scrutiny. One, in an edition of a few dozen, titled "2 ply constellation washing up for more than 10 months", consisted of a set of plastic plant pots filled with earth into which were embedded fragments of iron piping resembling grotesque cactus plants, each with a label attached. He defined this edition as a book, obtaining an ISBN for it and attempting unsuccessfully to get the British Library to accept a copy for their collection of UK books in print. Another edition, the "Boxes of Mein", consisted of dried noodles snugly packed into square cardboard boxes originally intended for storage of reel-to-reel audio tapes.

K and Robert had finally produced the sixth issue of *Alembic*, dedicated to David Miller, and next conceived the notion of making the seventh, the first to be produced at Lower Green Farm, an "Assemblage" issue. The idea was that contributors would produce their own pages. At the turn of the year they sent out invitations to around 60 artists and poets asking them each to send 200 copies of up to four A4 pages of work. The editorial process would consist simply of collating and staple-binding the resulting pages. In the event, 20 people sent in contributions. Paul Buck and Glenda George sent typed poems with the pages slit and stained. Tony Ward sent an A4 sheet with his name embossed on and a paper bag attached to it, in which nestled a little booklet with almost-not-there images on its pages. There were visual and sound-text poems by Paula Claire, Jeremy Adler, P C Fencott and Bob Cobbing.

Erik's own contribution was two sheets of sandpaper of different grades, sandwiching a flimsy A4 sheet. His interest, he said, was in the way the sandpaper abraded the middle sheet over time, producing delicate perturbations.

Robert, K and Erik took turns with the collating, walking round and round the kitchen table endlessly, the stacks of sheets very slowly diminishing even as the finished, assembled pile grew in height. Many days were spent doing this.

Erik also produced the wraparound cover for the issue, which was something of a tour de force. He did this on a massive cast-iron Albion press to which he had access, block-printing every single cover individually with the title "Alembic" in maroon and an abstract arrangement of black and grey blocks – no two covers of this issue of 200 copies were the same.

•

Other residents didn't tend to stay long at Lower Green Farm, nor did they participate in the artistic activities. A young Glaswegian called Sandy whose sole interests seemed to be beer and weed came and went. K mentioned to him that he was out of dope, and Sandy said he could score him some. He obtained a small bag of grass, which turned out at first blush to be rather a bad deal, consisting largely of seeds. But after the viable parts had been smoked K had the idea of planting some of the seeds in a clearing he had made in the overgrown garden at the back, and to his astonishment they started sprouting in no time at all.

A young woman, Nicolette, who knew people in Patchwork, moved in that spring. She may or may not have been a ballet dancer, or a would-be ballet dancer. Quite petite and attractive, she had firm dietary needs, mainly a requirement for regular steak. The friend who had helped her move was fascinated by Erik, and asked what living in Berlin was like, because she was thinking of moving there. Erik said he had enjoyed the city. Nicolette's friend asked why he enjoyed it, and he replied "Because it's full of crazy people doing meaningless things."

Cris Cheek and Lawrence Upton turned up with their contributions for *Alembic* 7, and all went manic. Erik's manic side was activated by those two. They stayed the weekend. David Miller visited, accompanied by Norman, now over his ordeal and presumably having found somewhere to live. Erik taught everybody the game of Go: very simple rules but mind-bogglingly complex outcomes. That fascinated the household for weeks.

A couple of months later, Nicolette had found somewhere else to live, with her boyfriend, and gave in her notice.

Her replacements, who stayed for a bit longer, were Steve and Tomo, who were mime artists. As with Erik and Muthis, they were recruited via an advert appealing for people to join a creative community. He was English, she Japanese. He spoke no Japanese at all and her English was rudimentary – she was in fact silent most of the time, although smiled a lot – but they seemed inordinately fond of each other, and communicated mainly in mime. They were extremely chilled-out and very calming to be with. They would sit together pointing at things that were happening, sometimes imitating them, or touching each other, and were very happy just doing so. They liked the black kitten Erik and Muthis had acquired, particularly because it was called Neko, which is "cat" in Japanese. It attacked its shadow and turned somersaults.

A few weeks after they arrived, they were banned from the local pub, the very same establishment in which the barman had undergone self-mortification for the accidental solecism of serving a half pint in a stemmed glass to a gentleman. There had been complaints. They were accused by the landlord of mocking the other customers, specifically, of holding them up to ridicule by imitating their movements; but there was an element of racism in this, the household generally agreed, because it was not just a case of customers offending other customers by imitating them but a *Japanese person* in an unusually close and unnatural liaison with an Englishman doing so, which would have been considered beyond the pale, beyond any pale this quiet suburban neighbourhood might have considered. Tomo for herself was phlegmatic about it, as she was about most things. She seemed happy. When it was her turn to cook, she spent many hours preparing an exquisitely delicious Japanese meal; by the time it was ready to come to table, though, some of the others in the household had taken to bread and cheese to stave off their hunger pangs. Steve explained they were whiling away the time at present, having been promised employment as extras, wearing chimpanzee costumes, on a new film version of *Tarzan*. In the meantime they were living on his SS and whatever scraps of work as mimes they might find, which were not plentiful in this neighbourhood. But filming had been delayed, so they just practised being chimps and honed their mimetic skills.

Then there was Marie. As before, it all started so well. She got on with everybody, she was enthusiastic and cheerful. A friend shipped over her stuff. She transferred her job to Croydon Pizzaland. But her status with K was unclear. Were they an item again or were they not? For a couple of nights, she shared K's bed. But there was no sexual chemistry. He felt uncomfortable about that. She gave no clue about what she was feeling, she was inscrutable. And he didn't know how to handle it. But he said it might be a good idea if she moved her things into the upstairs bedroom that had been allocated to her, where her own mattress had been put, and she complied without a word.

And so, like before, it started to unravel. After a few months, Marie started going missing. She was staying overnight with a friend, she would say sometimes. Or she'd just not turn up to the weekly house meeting. Then she started defaulting on her rent contribution. Another couple of months elapsed, and by now Marie was scarcely visible. Various members of the household expressed concern to K about "your girlfriend" who was not making any contribution of any kind, which was impacting on the finances apart from anything else. K said that she was not his girlfriend but that he would undertake to address the problem. He peeked in her by-now-abandoned room. It was a mess. Not until he viewed Tracey Emin's Bed at the Tate many years later did he witness the like. The only furniture was the mattress, with rumpled bedsheets; shoes, clothes and underwear were strewn around the floor everywhere, make-up items, Kleenex cartons and a few paperback books scattered about too, and many black bin-liners, still packed and half-spilling their contents. He went to meet her at Pizzaland in Croydon. She was uncommunicative. It was not clear where she was staying. She said she would move out of Lower Green Farm properly. She promised to pay the backlog she owed. She did turn up with some friends in a car to move her stuff out again, most of it still in the bin-liners it had arrived in. But she failed to pay any money. K wrote her an anguished letter, addressed to her at the Pizzaland branch, reiterating that he cared for her and for her wellbeing, but telling her he was under pressure from other members of the household to recover the debt she owed. It was not a letter he enjoyed writing, and he tormented himself about it for a long time afterwards. There was no reply.

•

K was now signing on at the Orpington SS office, so he no longer had to travel to London to claim his benefit. But the downside of this was there was greater focus on him – unlike in the inner city where the SS was a vast, non-productive factory where thousands of unemployed people like himself, an unwanted but also unregarded mass, turned up fortnightly to be automatically processed. No, They were now homing in on his particular job prospects. They were concerned about him.

They indicated that They were probing his situation. His situation interested Them. They were hassling him, in other words. He hadn't experienced such hassle for a long time. What were his aspirations? He said he was looking for a job in publishing or journalism. That was good, They said, he did have a degree after all, he should be admirably suited to and capable of looking after himself in such a placement. They promised to set him up with a job interview with the editor of the local paper. Well, that didn't happen, but the red light was beaming brightly and sinisterly. He had to find employment pretty soon.

He applied for a job with a local community bookshop, which sounded pleasant, but was turned down. Then he went for an interview for a half-time admin job for a small voluntary organisation working with homelessness projects in Camberwell, South London. To his amazement, he was offered it. His new employers added a condition, though, that he would have to learn to type properly. He declared he could already type two-fingered at an amazing rate, and on mimeograph stencils too, and demonstrated this; but if they wanted to send him to Pitman's stenographic school to learn proper touch typing, so be it. The salary was three thousand pounds a year, pro rata, which seemed an immense amount of money.

And so in January he started commuting: cycling from Lower Green Farm to Orpington rail station, travelling (with the bike stashed in the guard's van) by train to Brixton, cycling from there to the Cambridge House Settlement in the Camberwell Road. The people were nice, the work itself mostly dull but, in the context, socially useful.

His pleasure at attaining the job was a bit dented when someone in the tiny office revealed he had been one of only two candidates, the other having shown herself to be comprehensively incompetent.

He acquired his first ever credit card. It was green and red, and said ACCESS on the front. He could buy stuff on tick now. He had re-entered the official world.

•

Cooing wood pigeons and other sundry bird/machine noises jump-start K's day off work. A view of the jungle through latticed glass. Lower floor of the house pretty dark still. The morning paper in the porch, no mail yet. Everybody else still in bed. Chain on the blue front door. Breakfast – they all trickle down eventually, reading the paper at the table, passing pages from hand to hand. A weird but sunny day, with the familiar smell. Re-digging the vegetable plot in a clearing on the south-western side of the house, the soil sifted to a fine tilth and padded down in that section reserved for the seedbed. And fat glistening earthworms discovered, writhing in their writhy way. All very good. Marrow, tomato seedlings and, interspersed, those *cannabis sativa* shoots that made Robert so nervous. So then into London, change at London Bridge for Charing Cross and thence on the bus to Camden Town, where Compendium Bookshop is located, purchase of the new Oxford University Press edition of Basil Bunting's *Collected Poems* being the goal, and other sundry items too. Exchanging old, no longer wanted rock LPs at the Record Exchange for albums by Gato Barbieri, Dollar Brand, and also Don Cherry's *Eternal Rhythm*. Rest a little. A woman selling *Newsline* in the street, taking pity on her, and also being unusually optimistic today about the Revolution, buying a copy. She gives the V sign, not the rude one, the other way around. Golden liquid flooding London's western horizon at the end of the day, squeezing between commuters. Grey outlines of churches, offices, warehouses. Girders. An English, Greek & Continental Bakery. Forgetting to buy some cake or something for dessert tonight. At Orpington station, a conversation with an immensely fat blonde young woman just come back from the coast on a day trip with her little daughter, looking for the right bus. Erik preparing a German-style supper tonight, with plenty of cold sausage and home-made pickle. Muthis and Robert are both taking theoretical driving lessons, so that they could drive theoretical cars, it is supposed. Merriment about this.

Poetry readings at King's College in the Strand – initiative of Eric Mottram. K and Robert meet there, K straight from work, it's Tom Pickard reading on this occasion. Later, in the pub after it's all over, Erik turns up in the Citroen, in time to drive them all home to Lower Green Farm. On the way, he spies a discarded cable-drum and insists on stopping to pick it up for possible use, upturned, as a table. Two blokes watching from the shadows, causing both K and Robert some nervousness now, but they make no move, and the car continues on its way, the cable-drum squeezed into the back seat.

At the NFT cafeteria the next weekend, sharing cold steak pie and mixed salad with David Miller, who has a new woollen shoulder bag and talks enthusiastically about *Let Us Now Praise Famous Men*, which he urges K to read. And who should join them but Norman, and they have a conversation about Australian painters, a subject on which K is poorly informed.

K's old mate Keith sends an audio-cassette letter from Halifax, in which he mentions that he has met up with Jeff Nuttall (in connection with his work with that alternative theatre troupe), and that Jeff Nuttall has particularly praised K's poetry.

K is participating in a reading at a theatre in Kingston upon Thames, a benefit for *Tangent* poetry magazine, where he is mistakenly introduced as Ken Smith. But a plain and very nice girl comes up to him afterwards and says how much she enjoyed his performance. A blues band plays, fronted by Paul A Green, who is the near namesake of the mysterious and reclusive man that edits *Spectacular Diseases* magazine, and who declaims poetry with gusto and plays alto sax in the energetic but disorganised fashion of Captain Beefheart.

Des and June have now moved their household to Kingston upon Thames, to their new, permanent Patchwork community home, the short-life days at last over; and so when the reading's done K goes to visit their brand new house, marvels at it, and at the end of the evening kips down overnight in a sleeping bag among the various cats and dogs that are wandering about.

Back at Lower Green Farm, the vegetable garden in the clearing is coming on. The *South London Press* declaims that IT'S NEVER TOO LATE TO FRAME YOUR MELONS.

•

That summer, Robert, Erik and K organised three Saturday Courses at Lower Green Farm. The idea, which originated with Robert, was this: that on three successive Saturdays a notable Interesting Poet would give a day-long talk or series of talks on a topic of their choice; the events to be advertised with an admission charge attached to cover a reasonable fee for the poet plus the cost of catering for lunch, which would be in the hands of Erik.

Because K now had a proper job in London, the bulk of the work fell to Robert and Erik, though in truth there wasn't that much to it in the end, and the courses ran very smoothly.

So about a dozen or more people turned up at Lower Green Farm, almost all having made the journey from London, on the morning of the first Saturday, and there was a great deal of animated talk as they found their places. They included Maggie O'Sullivan, who arrived with Herbert Burke, an artist and concrete poet of North American origin – Maggie was notable for being one of the few women at this time participating in the London experimental poetry scene, having done time with Bob Cobbing's Writers Forum gatherings and starting a small press of her own. Geraldine Monk was another, and Carlyle Reedy too, though her appearances in public were rare. Maggie was from Lincolnshire originally, and the accent was retained in trace form in her voice, but she had Irish ancestry, which showed in her appearance: her dark curls and pale skin and eyes. Cobbing was there too, and the usual crowd were well represented: Cris, Ulli, Clive Fencott.

They were there to hear Allen Fisher, the first poet in the series. The talk took place in the spacious, panelled living room with the latticed windows giving on to the overgrown garden. Allen, a slim, wiry South Londoner who had befriended Eric Mottram and entered academia late in life, having spent time until then, in his own wry words, "selling dustbins", had a chart set up to which he added words gradually during the course of the day's proceedings. His movements jumped between the energetic and the calm.

The first word was SURVIVAL. And then followed STRUCTURE and FORM. Through STRUCTURE (that which remains constant) and FORM (related to feelings and emotions) he said we arrive at SURVIVAL. Or bone (structure) and blood (form) reaching to brain (survival). As he talked, he added other, triggered words, taken from punched cards, in a spontaneous architecture around these: procedure, perception, being, purpose, feeling, flux, necessity. Also memory. He spoke about "inventive" and "consistent" memory. He said that perception itself was a pattern-making procedure. The order in which he read the words that ended up on the chart he called "process". This dynamic of procedure on the one hand and process on the other was something of vital importance in his work as a poet and as an artist. He referenced Jackson Mac Low, and Raymond Roussel's *How I wrote certain of my books*, and also Louis Zukofsky, who said that poetry convinces by the form it creates, not by argument. He ranged widely through physics and psychology. He spoke about his use of music by Bach, Beethoven and Stockhausen as structural grids for his poetry. He spoke about mistakes, and their importance. About what he called "conscious mistakes" (relating maybe to Freud's slips) and their role in making non-repeatable structures. We should be, he said, more conscious of our own established structures, in order to be able to change them, which was why he distrusted automatic writing. Because feelings should be organised and given direction, not merely expressed. Made visible. And all of this that he was presenting was nothing other than a survival kit. Blood Bone Brain. Egyptian hieroglyphs of a jug of blood (the heart), a bone (structure) and an eagle, representing the brain, in its "place", which is the highest point of its range. But I'm not talking, he concluded, about three bottles on a table but a river on the table.

It was dense and glorious at times, but you could see the spaces it opened up. The people present seemed to indicate that the first Saturday Course had been an immense success which sent them home thinking and talking.

The next protagonist in this series, the following Saturday, was Eric Mottram. He had been very important to K as a teacher and mentor, as he was to many others. The first ever Reader in American Studies at London University, he had been K's tutor for a year when he was an undergraduate at King's College, later becoming a friend. His talk ranged widely across disciplines, and reflected his brilliance as a teacher.

And the third and final one was Bob Cobbing, who spent his entire Saturday *doing* poetry and sound rather than talking about it. He did this thing of gazing, of seeing through the medium of his tongue and throat, interpreting marks on the page, images onscreen, even the various household objects that he encountered in his wandering around the room, translating them into his own private language which he uttered, with great volume at times – but he was never a theorist. The only theoretical pronouncement he uttered in that booming voice, which he repeated in different ways at different points, was that every effort should be taken to make your poem "more like it is". Which actually was quite as profound as it was enigmatic.

But these two latter presentations were hugely overshadowed for K by what happened in the week after Allen Fisher's talk.

•

On the Monday afternoon, he received a phone call at work to say that Marie had been found collapsed in the street in Croydon and had been rushed to the intensive care unit at the Mayday Hospital, Thornton Heath.

He spent most of the evening then on the phone, finally making contact with John W, who had been hard to reach. John said he had been told by the hospital that Marie had very little chance of pulling through. She was on a respirator and there was no change at present in her condition. It was still unclear whether this was the result of a drug overdose, or something else.

A strange thing happened: Muthis gave K an unopened letter addressed to Marie that had been used as a bookmark in one of her books, which evidently Marie had once borrowed. K opened it. It was from a friend of Marie's called Wendy. It was rather pathetic, recalling good times, asking Marie to come round and visit her. K didn't know what to do. He did not remember this girl. He ended up returning the letter with a covering note explaining what had happened. But what was to happen, that he didn't know. Except that he thought she would die, and she did, lasting until Friday without regaining consciousness. It had been confirmed that cause of death was thought to have been a paracetamol overdose, but there would be an inquest.

On the train to London, K opened Edward Young's poem "Night Thoughts" and came upon

> Our dying friends come o'er us like a cloud,
> To damp our brainless ardours, and abate
> That glare of life which often blinds the wise.
> Our dying friends are pioneers, to smooth
> Our rugged pass to death; to break those bars
> Of terror and abhorrence Nature throws
> Cross our obstructed way; and thus to make
> Welcome, as safe, our port from every storm....

Marie's funeral took place twelve days later at an anonymous and gloomy cemetery in North London. It was a mild and overcast summer's day. There were eight mourners. K's mother accompanied him. John W was there in his dark grey three-piece suit and a black tie, and with him his friend, the headmistress of the school Buttercup attended. Robert came, blessings to him, and blessings also to June, who turned up by herself, apologising that Des, who had wanted to come, was at the last minute otherwise engaged with work. This strangely variegated little ensemble was rounded off by Marie's social worker and an elderly woman who apparently was a friend of the couple who had once fostered Marie as a child. Marie's colleague from the Pizza Express, a girl called Maureen, couldn't attend because there was a crisis on there, but had sent flowers. The ceremony was perfunctory, the grave that had been opened up was cavernous, Marie's coffin being lowered into position by silent gravediggers into a niche two or three layers down among other already existing incumbents. And that was that. One or two of the other mourners asked K for copies of a photograph of Marie that he had shown around. Then they slowly dispersed. K said goodbye to his mother at the train station and returned to Lower Green Farm with Robert.

Many times then and later K tried to discover what it was he was feeling, particularly at the moment the plain wooden box containing Marie's remains was lowered into its slot: grief, regret, sadness, guilt? None of these came to the fore. What he basically felt was no feeling, a sort of profound numbness. There was a feeling of no feeling right at the bottom of it, and this troubled him, because he thought strongly there should be a feeling. He went back to work the following day, and said no more about it to his work colleagues but instead immersed himself in the minutiae of running the small organisation housed in the attic offices of Cambridge House, Camberwell. In odd intervals at the office between doing paid work, he wrote fragments of poems in his notebook but they were contingent on day-to-day existence, they related to nothing in particular.

Meanwhile, news had come through that Greg Moore, founding father of Patchwork, had been killed in a car crash in Wales. This had thrown the whole of Patchwork into turmoil. It was not clear what the future held for the housing association. Most of the staff and many residents went to his funeral, held in Cardiff the day after Marie's.

•

K's diary entry for 16 July: This life is not real.

•

But life went on at Lower Green Farm, although the house was underpopulated during the summer months that followed. After the Saturday Courses were over, Robert went off for four weeks to teach at a university summer school. Erik and Muthis went travelling for a while in the old Citroen. Steve and Tomo remained. K booked himself a September holiday in Sicily with a friend from work.

On everybody's return in the autumn, plans were made for another issue of *Alembic* magazine, the eighth. This one was to be edited by K, with Erik on printing duties. Erik now had a new job: as Patchwork's official printer, no less. He had left War on Want, and was to be based at Lower Green Farm for this role; so the offset litho machine that belonged to Patchwork and that had resided in John W's office, the Hampstead Centre as was, would now be transported in a van and set up in the farmhouse kitchen, where, once reconditioned, and when it was not being used to produce Patchwork literature, reports and letterheadings, it could have an ancillary and unofficial function serving the creative doings of Lower Green Farm. But there were still costs involved, and the Greater London Arts Association after a very long time of waiting turned down *Alembic* for further grant aid – they had probably hated the "assemblage" issue – so there had to be a plan B for this to happen. And also K's time was more and more being tied up by the day job, and the travelling for it, and there were long waits also for contributors to deliver what was promised – a section of translations of contemporary poetry from other languages was planned, but the translators were slow and permissions late in coming – so all in all it was a veritable pain in the arse. Even though it was a good issue in prospect. It had work by Eric Mottram (elegies for Zukofsky, Brian Catling – who wasn't dead – and Jackson Pollock), and Lyn Hejinian and Rae Armantrout from among the new US poets, translations of Anne-Marie Albiach by Keith Waldrop and Heiner Bastian by Rosmarie Waldrop, of Reverdy by Peter Robinson and of a couple of Peruvian poets by David Tipton, and more work by Anna Couani, Joy Matthews and Opal L Nations. The unusual (for this time) prevalence of women among the contributors seemed to signify a certain political deliberation. The issue would not actually appear for another six months, funded in the end by personal contributions from Robert and K and from Peter, their erstwhile co-conspirator in the original *Alembic* project. And it would turn out to be the final issue.

But now autumn and winter were once more drawing closer, and there was the prospect again for K of never seeing the sun, of getting up in darkness, cycling to the station in grey light, the train ride in those clanking, slam-door carriages smelling of stale tobacco smoke, and then the impact of the Camberwell Road, and a day's work shut up in the office, and returning in renewed darkness via train and bicycle from the station, and then the same again the next day.

And meanwhile, there was correspondence from new poetry friends in America: Charles Bernstein and Bruce Andrews sending over regular issues of their new magazine which they called *L=A=N=G=U=A=G=E*, with the equals signs between the letters which made it hard to type on a typewriter, but which carried copious and vigorous exchanges of views, burrowing down into why we write, what is "writing" anyway, how do the words we set on the page signify, how do they relate to the "real" world if there is a "real" world that we can access outside of human discourse; and beyond that the politics of it all, the politics of the word and of the exchange of words and of the value entailed in those transactions... so K thought, why is this not happening here in this country, why do we go on writing our poems and reading our poems out loud in the upper rooms of London pubs that have the cheapest beer, because that seems to be the main criterion for choosing those venues, not the acoustics or ambient lighting, and never questioning why we write or how we write or what we write, and never a word whether of approbation or inquiry afterwards but a grunt or two, and then everybody goes to the bar and forgets about it all? And anyway, thought K, it's not about poems or Poetry with a capital P specifically, it's about writing with a lower-case w and also a w for why and what makes it work and what does working mean. So while he was waiting for the problems entailed in the eighth issue of *Alembic* to be resolved, and in between times devoted to the day job, he went back to his old Roneo duplicator, which was still serviceable, just about, intending it to be the vehicle for his new interim project, which was to be a kind of poetry newsletter, a successor in some respects to *Poetry Information*, but with poetry itself rather than news about it to be the main focus, poetry *as* news but also not excluding commentary on poetry and poetics and politics and reviews of new poetry books, and this to be produced cheaply and very quickly like a newspaper. He resolved to run off ten stencils every month (often having been typed at work piecemeal in the odd ten-minute interval), staple the printed, collated results at the top-left-hand corner and post them to a mailing list he compiled of about forty or so interested people, soliciting donations and subscriptions to defray the minimal costs. This new, interim magazine, that is to say, to be produced in the interims between issues of the real magazine, he called *Reality Studios*. And it was to, but he didn't know this, way outlive *Alembic* and last for ten years before morphing into something else. The name was taken from William Burroughs' *Nova Express*: "With your help we can occupy The Reality Studio and retake their universe of Fear Death and Monopoly" (signed Inspector J Lee of the Nova Police), which had been reappropriated by the Situationists as the endearingly ambitious spray-painted slogan "Storm the Reality Studios and retake the Universe" – endearingly ambitious anyway when re-reappropriated for a mimeographed poetry publication being mailed to approximately forty addresses. But you have to start small. What he was trying to invent, in short, was a blog or a webzine – hampered by the inescapable fact that there would be no such thing as the internet for another twenty years.

•

Did you send your stories to my agent, then? That was Jonathan, on the phone. Yes, said K, he'd spent much of the summer retyping his short stories. Because he'd given up yet again on writing that novel and had decided maybe he had accumulated enough stories, some of which had been in magazines and anthologies, to build a small book. Just about, perhaps. He was going to call it *Spontaneous Combustion in the Modern World*. He'd asked Jonathan for the address of his agent, which Jonathan had provided, and Jonathan had also promised to put in a word for him. But so far – and it had been a few weeks now – this agent had not replied. Jonathan had some good news of his own. He'd had another story in *Vogue*, and now *Vogue*, evidently deeming him the business, had commissioned him to, wait for it, interview David Bowie. Yes, that was right. He was to be flown to Glasgow to do this – why Glasgow was not clear, maybe Bowie needed to be caught in the midst of a tour and that was the only opportunity. Wow, said K. And that was not all: Harvester Press had, after some shillying and some shallying, agreed to publish one of Jonathan's novels. That was great for Jonathan, K said. He was on his way.

•

Things were no longer the same. A wee bit of tension had infiltrated into the household, just a smidgeon. It had previously been felt when Marie had gone AWOL and stopped paying her share of the rent and there'd been some reference, in respect of K, to "your girlfriend". Well, it wasn't much, but it was there. And now it returned. An observation had been made, just an observation in passing, that K happened to occupy the largest bedroom, actually the second of the two panelled rooms on the ground floor, and there was only one of him, whereas Erik and Muthis were a bit pushed for space in their bedroom on the first floor, which was quite a big bedroom but not as big as that other room. Which K happened to occupy, because he had claimed it, being the first person (apart from the abortive case of Norman) to occupy the premises. Well, K brooded over that mention, and then he said OK, I'll move rooms, and they said oh no no, we didn't mean that, but it had been meant, or something had been meant.

And then what happened next is that there had been an application at K's workplace for renewed and expanded funding from the London Boroughs of Lambeth, Southwark and Lewisham, because the project to bring together disparate voluntary organisations working with single homeless people in South-East London under a single umbrella, providing for shared resources and expertise, had been pretty successful, and those who knew reckoned there was a good chance of a funding expansion. And this would provide for posts to be regraded, including K's part-time post, the proposal being that it be upgraded to the equivalent of Council Officer status, full-time, so that if this was successful, which the signs were it would be, his income would triple, but then he would have to work every day of the week in his new capacity as an unofficial Officer. Well, this came to pass, and K was offered the full-time post at an enhanced grade, with benefits, and who could say no to that? But K thought, I can't bear to commute every single day from way out there in the sticks into the inner city, every single fucking day of the week.

But the solution stared him in the face then, because one of his new work colleagues lived in, and indeed had been a founder member of, a radical housing co-operative just down the road from the office, the Balfour Street Project, which was to be found off the Old Kent Road, near the Elephant & Castle. This colleague said they were looking for new tenants: what was happening in this hitherto short-life housing co-op in a terrace of seven or eight houses, was that there were also plans to renovate the block at the end of the street, called Railway Buildings, and put in eight purpose-built flats, and did he want to apply for one of those? They would be permanent tenancies. He asked around, and it seemed this housing co-op was well thought of, though everybody added "they're very *political*". That was all right. And bloody hell, it was a bare twenty minutes' walk from the office in the Camberwell Road and maybe eight minutes, if that, on the bike. So he was interviewed by a panel from the housing co-op, which did not include his work colleague, but included maybe one other from the house the colleague shared, and they were all very nice. They said they'd like to have him, they liked what he had to say, and he would be allocated a flat just as soon as one became available.

So now he found himself, for the second time in two years, breaking the news to his fellow householders that he would be giving in his notice, in this case moving out of Lower Green Farm, as soon as a space was available in the housing co-op in London.

As it turned out, it wouldn't be quite as simple as that. Because of the complexities, there was a lengthy hiatus in which K moved out of his room into another room within Lower Green Farm, allowing Erik and Muthis to occupy the largest room, and there were also murmurings meanwhile from Patchwork about the status of the licence and whether and when Bromley Council might be requiring the house back, presumably to demolish it, because the M25 London orbital road was definitely coming.

K spent some of his remaining time in the garden, that is to say, the little clearing in the thick undergrowth behind the house in which he had attempted to grow vegetables. He recalled there had been a mad plan to keep chickens in one of the two large outhouses that were otherwise never used, until it had been realised nobody had the least idea how to do such a thing and everybody felt squeamish at the idea of wringing chickens' necks which apparently you had to face if you didn't want an increasing number of elderly non-laying birds on your hands. He harvested the remainder of the crop, starting with the marijuana plants which had been causing Robert so much anxiety because they were ill-concealed by the tomato plants that had been carefully planted around them, in fact, had way outstripped them in growth – they were magnificent specimens, of a heady pungency in their aroma, six sturdy children standing proud. They were the scarcely believable result of the handful of seeds K had sown, rather haphazardly and without too much thought, the residue of that bad deal he had scored from Sandy all those months ago, mostly sticks, stems and seeds, which had now undergone the vegetal equivalent of transition from ugly duckling to swan. Not only did they make magnificent plants, but when chopped in their prime like John Barleycorn, lifted and pegged upside down on a line in an outhouse to dry for a couple of weeks, and then collected and the dry leaves crumbled, and rolled into joints and smoked, well, their effect on the head was wondrous indeed.

Time went on, K started the full-time job, still attempting to commute, and that secure tenancy he'd been offered had not yet materialised. So then his colleague said, Why don't you come and live in our shared house in the co-op while you're waiting, we've got a room vacant? Not another shared house, thought K, but there were few other options, and eventually he'd get his flat, so he agreed. And the great relief of returning to London, that was so powerful.

After K had moved out, there was a kind of domino effect. The Project was effectively dead – it had lasted a bare eighteen months, but there were few regrets. Robert had himself been offered full-time employment, an academic job teaching English at Royal Holloway College. He moved to a bedsit in West Hampstead, the landlord of which was a former schoolfriend of Harold Pinter. All his time for the next few months was taken writing lectures; the issue of *Alembic* he had been meant to edit, the one following K's, took a back seat, and then a seat even further back as his work duties encroached further, and finally was abandoned, and the poetry magazine was no more.

That *Tarzan* movie in which Steve and Tomo were going to be chimps appeared to have been postponed indefinitely and they never got the call. So eventually, after several months at Lower Green Farm, there being no other work immediately available for two mimes, they decided to go and live in Japan instead for an unspecified period.

Erik and Muthis moved back to London, occupying the basement of a tall, semi-derelict house in Islington shared by Ulli, now Freer and no longer McCarthy. K visited them frequently there, and subsequently taped a long series of interviews with Erik, the transcript of which was published as part of *Reality Studios*.

K was now living with his work colleague and *his* housemates in the communal house on Balfour Street, and biking to work every day through the back streets to Camberwell Road. It was not like the Sunderland Terrace household. It was much smarter. Although the four others sharing the house were indeed pretty left-wing, being involved in various trade union or Labour Party or feminist activities, they also liked their comforts, such as new fitted carpets and sofas and good lighting and nice curtains from John Lewis and good food and wine. But also they were very receptive to K's stash, the mortal remains of those six fine children, now accommodated within two or three jam jars. They were very kind to him. All his books were now packed and stacked in cardboard boxes because the room he occupied was too small to accommodate them. He began to get a sense of the internal politics of the housing co-op he was now part of. The whole question of moving to permanent tenancies in refurbished accommodation, in partnership with a charitable housing association, was a source of heated argument. In various camps were the household he'd befriended and their allies, who championed this plan; and a group of others who were puritanically committed to getting one's hands dirty plastering and bricklaying and mending roofs and who distrusted what they regarded as bourgeois aspirations; and then maybe a third group who just wanted to get on with their lives and had no interest in ideological battles of this kind and had to be endlessly cajoled into making some kind of contribution. The short-life flat he had now been promised, as a prelude to that eventual long-term tenancy, was on hold, because the space that had been anticipated hadn't materialised because the couple who were meant to be moving out, the original founders of the Balfour Street Project, who had after many years fallen out with every single one of the other members, in every camp, had been unable to find a place to move to and were continuing to occupy their house but not speaking to anyone. But that was OK. Things he had hoped for would come to pass eventually.

K tried to continue with his writing as best he could, and also cranked out ten pages of *Reality Studios* every month on the Roneo, which was somehow squeezed into a corner of his room, an eccentricity that was regarded with fond indulgence by his new housemates. They said: Why on earth don't you join our communal household permanently? We all like you, they added. No, he said, that's all right, but I think I still want my own flat. Where I can be myself. Whoever that is. He became involved with the union at work. He volunteered to manage the admin and rents for the co-op, because everybody was obliged to put in so much work every month, and he preferred that to bricklaying in the rain. It was fine for the time being. It was another Project.

A nest full of eggs

Every day the future comes nearer; every single day that passes, and they pass much more quickly now, it approaches; but it gets no clearer, no more decipherable than at the beginning – the beginning? – what I mean to say is, at the time when I was closer to the beginning, when my senses were more rudimentary. And now as I bring myself to write this, in many ways it gets more difficult, because I am no longer relying on those long-ago set-down accounts of what happened, and when, and wherefore, etc etc; no longer building on those familiar narratives but on the thin air of now. You know, like the cartoon character running from some assailant towards the cliff edge and continuing to run beyond, without noticing for a short while thereafter that there is nothing to support his pattering little feet until he looks down and then of course the shock of awareness, of seeing for the first time the yawning space beneath him, provokes his belated downfall. It's a familiar trope, perhaps rather hackneyed by now, but an apt one I think. So anyway the awful thought comes that the future, outside the frame, is actually *down there*. And looking back, well, all of that seemed solid at the time, more or less in focus, and there was a lot of it to build on, but still, it's now slipping out of reach. Not forgetting that the time to come is far less capacious, I mean there is less of it. So I'd better hurry, or it will be used up.

Not forgetting. That's the thing. That would be good. How can we imagine the future if we have no access to the past?

The future can only ever be imagined. It never arrives. It can be brought to mind by being out of mind, by stepping off the clifftop of memory. Oh, such tedious metaphors – enough. I only have, as my resource, autobiographical memory, which is telling a story, which is in essence a pattern-making activity, a creative response to events that have occurred, or may have occurred. The neurologists tell us that memories are not records stored in the filing cabinet of the brain, waiting over the years to be retrieved. They are built anew each time we try to retrieve them, when we create a mental representation on the fly of something that may or may not have happened, but somehow has left its mark. A trigger can activate the representation by firing a node in the network in which the sources are encoded and which connects them . Memories are, say the neurologists, about optimising decision-making in the future. But there is no guarantee they represent verifiable facts. They are distributed widely in the brain across interconnections, with immense potential for interference. When they lapse, it is not because storage space is at a premium. They fade when the connections degrade. I am reminded of the difficult last years experienced by my wife's father, who struggled as he entered his nineties to piece together the remnants of his memories while coping with the frayed interconnections in his brain that would have assisted the pattern-making; and how he tried to create new patterns that didn't make any sense but at least enabled some kind of temporary stringing-together that would hold for now. It was especially poignant as he had the reputation of being a storyteller, in his prime holding audiences fascinated with his tales of life in rural Norfolk before the Second World War, an activity he called "yarning" that had a tradition in the annals of the family, for one of his uncles had been a raconteur, with a fund of texts he had written that, when performed for entertainment in the evenings, he had called "recitations", texts that after he died his widow had burned, for reasons never explained; and another uncle had actually written books about life as a mole-catcher and a railway signalman in the Fens which had become popular, and he had appeared on regional television in the 1970s in a regular series of programmes on rural life, being interviewed wearing collarless shirt and neckerchief, a faux-rural garb foisted upon him by the programme makers which he would never have worn in real life. And so my wife's father had carried on the tradition, keeping family and friends entertained and amused with his yarning, until his brain cells started to die and the pattern-making began to strain credulity. He would ring us up, worried that his wife's (my wife's mother's) bicycle was not to be found in the garden shed, deducing from this that she had been held up at work for some inexplicable reason, what could it possibly be? and had to be gently reminded that the bicycle had gone very many years ago and that his beloved wife had died almost as many years ago, and the world he was attempting to re-create had not existed in reality in all that time.

In memory, the world is created – re-created – every day, every single moment, becoming new again, bringing into existence the possibilities of new futures, in a fluid state, enhancing survival. Memory is a catastrophic breaking-free, a benign catastrophe, if you will. As suggested by the poet and artist Allen Fisher, who makes an appearance in the pages you have just been reading, and who remains to this day a friend of mine, it is a vital component of the pattern-making we need to do each day as a means of surviving – knowing about it and knowing how we know. With its loss or degradation, all the principalities and echelons of existence are obliterated, their hierarchies flattened, their glitter dispersed, and time shatters to its atoms, its instances separated out so that they can no longer be inspected from front to back and back to front again and be seen as cohesive, as elements in a system that can be worked with and worked through.

But what of those many pages that bring us up to this point? Where are these vaulted spaces they try to conjure? What is the time that is being evoked? I seem to remember it, anyway, whether through inventive or consistent memory. It is a good forty years since the events that inspired this narrative actually occurred, and the evidence for them is naturally incomplete. So I have laboured to complete the narrative by discovering or inventing connections, trying to fill the gaps with consistent or invented memories, vainly as it happens, because the more you fill in the more new gaps appear, triggering new memory-connections, fractally self-similar, a process, as I have already surmised, that could extend infinitely – within the unknown constraints of the capacity of the human mind anyway – so when might you call a halt and say this is ridiculous, what is the point? Has the point, if there is one, been made? Has it even been reached?

But then of course the realisation becomes apparent: that the gaps that appear, and keep on appearing in new places however much you toil to fill them, are inevitable and necessary. As Edwin Muir has written of Kafka: "We know the end he had in mind for all his stories; but the road to it could have gone on forever, for life as he saw it was endlessly ambiguous; so that there seems to be a necessity in the gaps which are left in his three stories [*The Trial, The Castle* and *America*]; if he had filled up these gaps, others would have appeared." The process is inexhaustible, that is why it is called process; the framing is arbitrary, the decision to allow ellipses, and in particular the big ellipsis that occurs at the very end of the narrative, to be themselves, has to be made at some point decided by the author because there is no objective point of completion, not ever, no closure, to use a now fashionable word. And then the story can breathe, and live on, live with its indeterminacies, transferred from the imagination of the author to the imagination of the reader and left in safe-keeping there to be done with as the reader may wish.

And the obvious corollary to all this is the medium itself of the narrative, the question of the language with which it is conveyed, for it needs a conveyance of some kind and I'm doing the best I can here. All I have at my disposal to render these events or my take on these events, which may or may not have happened, is the words you are reading right now, but what are these double entities of moving air and reposing ink? They are slippery and elusive, they do not always mean what you think they mean, their relation to those long gone or imagined events is not simple, their relation to you, reader, is not simple. Their tendency to take over and obscure some imagined truth vies with their purported aim of rendering that truth plain and simple. Poetry is involved in that business, of course, but I'm not going into that here; perhaps I'll return to it later. At any rate, language, like that other system known as the scientific method, is a different world from the world of the real, it's a code that enables glimpses of how someone might imagine the real, and thereby have some dealing with or accounting for it, but the real is not really here, and maybe it's the place I now only dimly remember, where the talking dead are – or is it the place where I am now as I write or where you are now as you read these words, as you turn the page, either physically taking up the edge of the paper and flicking it over or else commanding this movement electronically with a sweep or tap of your finger?

•

It is forty years or more, as I've said, since the events described in the preceding pages of this book. I am writing in a house within the boundaries of the Borough of Hastings, on the south coast of England, in the second decade of the twenty-first century. More than half the time that's elapsed has been shared with the person now dearest to me, my wife. I can hear her distantly in her music room practising scales and exercises on the soprano saxophone as I sit here in my study tapping out these words on the computer. It's a winter morning as I first-draft this; yesterday was deep grey, and at one point the light from the iMac screen was the only illumination in the room, but this morning has begun clear and bright; the sky, observable from the window on my left, a very pale blue, the brightness of the hidden sun haloing the block of flats that stands between us and the English Channel. We have been in this house a little over nine months now, having been fourteen years in the one that preceded this one. What is this beautiful house? It's an edifice that can provide an oasis of calm, the kind you need to create writing or music: the drone or pedal point that underlies whatever frenzy of the imagination may ensue. My writing room is in the basement, that's to say a floor and a half below street level at the front, but because the house is built on a sharp decline from the street there is a view and plenty of light obtainable through my window. The distant sound of the soprano sax has ceased for now. The peace is briefly and minimally interrupted, in peripheral vision to the left, by a squirrel skittering along the top of the wooden fence that marks the boundary of the small decking area outside the window – only a moment, and it's gone. Above my desk and to my right are closely packed bookshelves – they are not stacked on house bricks, but fastened to the walls – the far wall being devoted to poetry books that have been amassed in those forty-plus years. My acoustic and electric guitars and one of my bass guitars repose on stands on the solid, fake-wood floor. But ... how did I get here?

A reminder has popped up on my computer screen, as it does at set intervals, which simply says "write!" And on the noticeboard to the right of the screen is pinned a card with the slogan, under an image of a computer keyboard being squeezed by human hands, the keys scattering like drops of juice, WRITE NOW!

And so I do, but can only build it sentence by sentence, casting aside as best I can the shadow of a doubt that accompanies each as it emerges, slowly, making its minuscule difference between then and now and the thereafter that is as yet masked by silence. "Or walking towards that other, /" writes W S Graham, "The new step arrives out / Of all my steps taken / And out of today's light." Onward then, keeping the faith, which is in no sense to be confused with belief, because nothing is to be believed without good reason; the faith, then, that there is some way out of here, even when here is an insoluble mystery; and why would you want to be out of it anyway, why, because there's no satisfaction to be had staying put. I suppose that is the least that can be said. If nothing else other than to refute that bleak utterance, quoted by Hastings-based film-maker Andrew Kötting, of Eugene O'Neill: "There is no present or future – only the past, happening over and over again – now." It would appear so sometimes, were I only to switch on the TV to witness the seemingly eternal soap opera that is the enactment of the Will of the People as decreed by the self-serving and the plainly ignorant. And all the rest of that fucking nonsense. There must be some way out of here. So I write another sentence. There it is. How can another sentence make a difference to a life sentence? The question is of course posed by the Joker to the Thief. There is no answer, there never is, but you have to make as though everything depends on what would transpire were everything to be not as it is but as it might be. "Where would I go, if I could go," pleads a narrative voice as imagined by old Sam Beckett, "who would I be, if I could be, what would I say, if I had a voice, who says this, saying it's me?"

It's the selves that now clamour for attention, the serial personae that populate my brain, chimerae that flit onto and off the stage, bearing an uncanny resemblance to the person I have at times imagined myself to be: an opportunist witness, an angel of happenstance, a misled believer, an unfortunate wretch, even an agent sometimes, or on other occasions just a burglar in shammy leather, an opportunist who happened to be passing. These pages that are now stacking up, here, in what has become a book, this is where I met and/or created you, Citizen K; how convincingly I now see you played the part of the protagonist in his various semblances, between the ages, let's say, of twenty-four to twenty-eight, fumbling at will in various locations, from the faraway London of short-life housing and improbable make-do to New York, Chicago, Los Angeles, back to London, to the suburban wilds of Green Street Green and back yet again to London, depositing en route serial representations, psychic photographs, like that familiar vagrant observed before the narrative proper even began, from within the vortex induced by a pharmaceutical, whose ragged robe had become radiant, who trudged along the road (Chepstow Villas, it may have been, or possibly Artesian Road) depositing, as he trudged, different selves at each memory stage, the images of which lingered a while before slowly fading.

•

I had a dream in which there appeared a grand procession moving slowly down an urban hill that seemed to me terribly familiar, but also dreadfully strange; and this gathering turned out to consist in large part of everyone I'd ever known in my life. Which was exciting when I first realised this. It was not clear whether I was reviewing this procession in a leisurely and seigneurial way, nodding seriously like a generalissimo at the passing tributes to my person or to my function, whatever that was, or whether I was spectating from the sidelines as part of a crowd, or indeed was actually part of the procession itself, in the very midst of it, processing down the hill to wherever the ultimate destination might be. Or possibly I was not there at all, my self had been extinguished and this particular imagery had arisen out of nowhere creating an impression that was misleading.

Well, that dream happened before we moved house, and when we did I realised, or decided, that the hill, which had seemed as though it was probably a street in Hastings, perhaps that bit of Old London Road that comes down into the Old Town, or a part of The Ridge, or maybe it was in London, or on the Rock of Gibraltar, or wherever, was in fact the hill leading down to Warrior Square, St Leonards-on-Sea. And then it was as though my imagination reverse-engineered it in the light of that fancy, and I saw the images anew, all the people I had ever known, six or seven decades of them, processing solemnly down the potholed declination, past the Convent gardens, past Empress Coaches, past the refuse bins maybe with an abandoned sofa or mattress discarded at the roadside nearby from the flats being refurbished, past the Greek Orthodox church – though the exact landmarks are vague, because this is a dream (and anyway, it's all been reverse-engineered, so I'm making it up, frankly) – towards Warrior Square gardens, where the statue of Queen Victoria to the left is gazing stonily out to sea (on the mornings after Bank Holiday celebrations she sometimes wears a traffic cone on her head) and the sombre rose garden can be seen on the right, below which Jeremy Corbyn once addressed the faithful who shouted and whooped and sang White Stripes choruses and waved banners and placards. That was where the procession was heading. With what intention? Well, the dream's later stages released a welter of unwelcomeness: I mean, it all started to go wrong, in what precise way and how that started, that's not clear, but it wasn't going the way I expected or hoped for, the people I knew or had known, some loved some not so loved, seemed not to know me any longer, or at least one or more of them gave me a perfunctory nod at best, just an acknowledgement, sometimes it seemed to me a bit grudgingly, and I realised too that they came from a jumble of different experiences and different periods in my life, and if they appeared, as I said, no longer to know me, well, many of them, groups of them, didn't know each other at all, or only slightly, enough to cause awkwardness and social perils of every kind, and, because *I* was the connecting factor in all this, I was therefore the source of this particular awkwardness or lack of good faith that wasn't what was needed. Now, while I was pondering and trying to reconcile in my dream-brain all the different factions and world views and family loyalties represented there, it started to get really out of hand: first, there was the sound of military music welling up from somewhere, initially as a faint background and then getting louder and louder until it was unbearable, and then I saw the crowds had to start getting out of the way of this military band, which approached blaring out a military tune, "Colonel Bogey" or some such – it might have been the band of the Grenadier Guards or of the Royal Marines – and there were police and military weapons infiltrating the crowd, which started to become restive and to shout, at first in isolated calls and then more continuously, and I realised now I really *didn't* know these people, for the people I had known in my life even if slightly were slowly disappearing and people I didn't know at all were beginning to predominate; it was becoming intensely chaotic, there was more and more shouting, there was the crunch of boots on worn-out tarmac, the police appeared in numbers out of everywhere, a squadron of jet aircraft suddenly roared past overhead, and now people were fighting and running, weapons firing or flying, and I heard someone shouting "Let's get out of here!' which seemed sensible advice, except that all sensibility had vanished, and I, if I were still there, which wasn't clear – it wasn't exactly clear, as I've intimated, whether I had ever been there at all – thought that's a shame, that's a bitter shame, it could have come to something, but that's not going to happen now, whatever it was that it might have come to is not going to happen, by which I mean something good, some resolution that would have been the way out, something that would have been the outcome.

•

Why does the narrative break off where it does? This may be the most frequently asked question. The glib answer, and how we love glibness, because it's so sexy, is that it breaks when it stops making sense. Let the reader then make what sense s/he can. K's final diary entry is dated 26 September 1978, and ends: "At last we caught the bus to the airport, where we met the others. We flew home. A final vision of Etna towering blackly over Sicily like the shadow of death – then the Aeolian Islands now far below – then cloud. / England was cold." That was written at the conclusion of an Italian holiday, and then there is no more for at least eight years, a lacuna punctuated only by accounts of dreams from time to time. These take us into a different space altogether, one that has to be imagined.

So the space outside my study has changed. No longer do I see that wooden fence beyond the decking area along which my friend the squirrel sometimes scurries, from right to left and later back again, nor the grimy backs of the flats that obscure the view of the English Channel on the other side (better viewable from our upstairs balcony), but instead I observe a river of light, a river in flames, on which a small boat is foundering. I see my family on the boat, my dead parents and my living sister, maybe my own self, suffused by the golden, shimmering light, which I understand to be X-rays emanating from the burning river itself, making their bodies translucent, revealing their skeletons. I become afraid when I see them, not because of how they appear, but because I know I saw them only just now in another part of the house, apparently alive and well. I get on my bicycle and ride away from the house at breakneck speed. Now at last I am far away. I seem to have arrived in China, in the Mao era possibly, on a wide concourse filled with people moving hither and thither. I see men in business suits walking round in circles, and I am informed they are "practising self-criticism". I'm having my hair cut by a Chinese barber. When he's finished, I ride off once more on my bike, but then remember I left all my possessions, which had been in a saddle bag, behind in the barbershop. On returning, I find the barbershop has been abandoned, but my things can be seen in the sink, which is filled with water. I decide I have to make some money to survive; fortunately, Mrs J has bequeathed me her shop, but the premises are in a bad state of repair, with holes in the front wall below the windows, where the wind comes in. Also, it is very badly situated, no longer where I remember it but set back from the road and separated from it by a stone wall, and the area is very drab. Nevertheless, I have high hopes of success. The stock is partly Mrs J's old things, partly items salvaged from skips by my friend Des, and partly second-hand books. I lock up for the day and walk home through the anonymous streets of London, but I can no longer remember where home is, or how to get to it. All of a sudden, my attention is caught by a building fashioned somewhat like a circus big top; it turns out, when I enter it, to be a museum of sorts, enfolding a staged representation of some kind of long-ago Eden, populated by live animals, mostly African, which I can hear prowling around. I wander with trepidation through its darkened corridors, on the lookout for danger. A creature approaches: it is somewhat like an aardvark or armadillo, but it can converse in human language, and so I adopt it thankfully as a companion, and it guides me safely out of the building. I am still trying to find my way home. But now London, if this is where I am, has been transformed into a futuristic cityscape. Music by David Bowie is playing. The whole city has been frozen and people everywhere have been put into suspended animation for several decades, just as they were while driving their cars or walking along the street. But now they are gradually beginning to wake up. As they slowly come to their senses they find they have acquired amazing powers: for instance, of flight. The two of us, the animal I've befriended and I, watch as one silver-clad citizen cavorts in the sky like a trapeze artist without a trapeze.

•

When I look back on it, that period of my life that is the main subject of this narrative, mediated through the persona of K, encompassing no more than four years in all, itself seems like a dream with endless branchings. Let's consider the "poets" and their doings. The activities described here were close to the beginnings of what may now be termed the alt-poetry or avant-poetry scene, though of course nobody ever called it that or called it anything, why would we? But how did we survive? How did we make contact with each other? Without the instant and pervasive electronic communications of today, it seems chance encounters must have dictated events. And so they did. Consider for instance: K, trying to earn enough money to buy himself time to write and also disseminate poetry few people want to read, gets a casual part-time job working for an educational therapist who happens to have as his clients the Rock Star couple who have been told they must employ a tutor for their daughter for the duration of their next tour of the USA; he gets the gig; and by happenstance, while rendezvousing in Manhattan (where he finds himself as a result) with a girl his housemate once met (by chance) on the streets of London and gave temporary lodging to, she introduces him to her boyfriend who just happens to have invited to dinner the person who will be the editor of one of the influential presses of the Language writing movement, whom K now meets; and in this way a portal is opened up for poets of similar persuasion on either side of the Atlantic to converse. That is pretty weird. But that's how it was. No internet, no World Wide Web, no search engines, no email. You met someone, and they said, hey you should check out so-and-so, and they gave you that person's address, so you wrote them a letter. Or the word went round that a certain reading series in London or elsewhere was important, or certainly *interesting*, and you turned up to see what was going on. And someone at that reading would say, have you read so-and-so? No? all right, check out their books at Compendium Bookshop, or if you couldn't afford to buy books there was always the Poetry Library where you could borrow three or four at a time, take them home and read them. You couldn't search online, but there was always a wealth of news in *Poetry Information* or *Second Aeon* magazines, also available at Compendium or by postal subscription.

No overarching aesthetic theory appeared to underpin these exchanges. (Theory with a capital T was still in the future, though some few were already into the philosophies of the *Tel Quel* school and the like.) If poets talked about the ethos or the fundaments of their art, that was called *Poetics*, but poets, in Britain at least, rarely did. If you knew, you didn't talk. So it was not altogether clarified how or why our brains were creating these new spaces or new aesthetics, or how these were to be shared. All we knew is that we wanted to cross frontiers.

There were some common themes. The need to read aloud or to listen to poetry being read aloud was one of these, whether through heeding the strictures of Basil Bunting, one of the few English role models for these poets, whose sonorous (though some now say slightly faked) North Eastern vowels and resonating consonants were highly satisfying, or whether under the influence of Bob Cobbing and his cohorts who made sounds mysteriously out of graphic images on the page, or even off the page, booming and jittering, phonemes rippling like mad. Whatever space one might be in, or headed towards, whether maximalist, such as the all-encompassing architectures of Olson, or minimalist, such as the haiku-like restraint of Scotland's own Thomas A Clark or Ian Hamilton Finlay where it shaded into Concrete Poetry, whether the richness and strangeness of continental Surrealism or the anarchy and non-sequiturs of Dada, or the hermetic linguistic inventions of Paul Celan, or the radical and sophisticated appropriation of pop cultural modes and lingo epitomised by the New York School, it was all supremely exciting and offered multiple possibilities. This was the supposed "British Poetry Revival" that K dwelt on the fringes of in those days. Whatever our differences, though, we all knew, without needing to say it, what we were *against*: the tyranny of Official British Verse, as typified by the poets of The Movement with their fetish of plain speech and "communication", their harking back to the Georgians, or the Edwardians or whatever, back to an imagined Golden Age of English letters, their fear of innovation and foreignness, and their ever so politely framed derision directed towards the *different*.

Well, that was the poetry itself, but how to share it, beyond the confines of those dingy and ill-lit pub upper rooms where the rituals of poetry readings happened? Faber & Faber were unlikely to come waving fat contracts at any of these people. It was a question then of resorting to do-it-yourself methods of reproduction, and of necessity subscribing to a proto-punk aesthetic in this. For myself I rather admire the craftsmanship of those Fulcrum Press or Trigram Press letterpress or lithographically produced editions; and the poets associated with them in their pomp (the late Sixties to the late Seventies) were certainly held in awe by many who resigned themselves to the only means available, the messy old mimeograph or (later) the photocopier. So the short-lived magazines and the chapbooks and pamphlets and broadsides poured forth incessantly from every direction, and it was hard to keep up with this branching and splitting and fusing, the feuds and the alliances; no possible theory of branching could be devised to account for it all. Mostly the tribes did get on in rough symbiosis, though there was always news of, dare we say, warring clans – the town of Royston being, someone said, a frontier – and there were some who felt snubbed, in the way that happens, perhaps uniquely, in England, where nothing is said yet the absence of saying is more eloquent than any direct barb could be, but even then there was private understanding between individuals, there was acknowledgement of exceptions to unspoken rules, and always there were some individuals also who dwelt and worked in the interstices between such groupings and could not be assigned to one or the other.

With all this came an urgent need for survival, for how could one survive in a capitalist society, given the powerful urge to pursue ends that were not compatible with assumed notions of exchange value? But in some ways it was easier then than now, even with no money coming in: you could live cheaply, whether renting a furnished room or squatting or hanging on in short-life property which might be reclaimed in a year or so but there would always be another to go to, and there was always the resource of Social Security, or the SS as many referred to it because of the possibility they would come down hard on you out of nowhere, but generally there wasn't the immense, remorseless, dehumanised, roboticised bureaucracy that is so familiar today. The efficiencies of repression had not yet been perfected: that would be done by a combination of (in the UK) the politics of Margaret Thatcher (hers is the unmentioned ghost that haunts these pages, biding its time before the election of 1979) and information technological breakthroughs. But in the meantime there were niches you could hide in, and survive. You could get away with it much of the time, particularly if you didn't need a great deal to live on.

More even than economic survival was a mutual need for esteem where none was granted from above. Ah, that was a difficult one. The esteem had to be generated from ground level, and had to be won from others in the same position as oneself. A species of added value, entirely self-created, or created by the group, by means of self-bonding. Do I mean male bonding? Yes, I suppose I do. Revisionist historians of that period of alternative poetries, embarrassed by the lack of women on record as participating, may try to highlight the few that did, or make a case for exclusion of unknown women poets who might have been doing equally innovative stuff elsewhere but went unnoticed or were actively repressed, but the fact is that the majority of the innovative stuff was produced by men, and the question of active repression of women did not seem to arise, they just weren't around. It is true that, when a decade later than the era described here the anthology *A Various Art* was published, apparently celebrating a generation of poets arising out of and centred on the Cambridge explosion (rather than the London one, or the ones all around the country), the only woman included in a selection of seventeen was a dead one; and that Denise Riley, Wendy Mulford and Grace Lake, aka Anna Mendelssohn, for three, might have had a just claim, but were left out. But my London experience was that the few women participating were taken seriously and were encouraged (Bob Cobbing for one being exceptionally broad-minded and egalitarian in conducting his publishing and workshop programmes), but they were very few, there's no question about that.

Now to get back to male bonding, there was that, undoubtedly. By which I mean the boys' school ethos, whereby a boy may gain kudos from his pals for the choices he makes – which album to buy, which band to follow, etc, and in this context which poets or poetry schools are important – whereafter he may be admitted to the elite of those who know, those who may be consulted for advice as to further choices. A woman poet once designated this to me as homoeroticism, by which (she added, for clarification) she didn't mean homosexuality as such (the scene was pretty much white male hetero, and any private inclinations otherwise would have been kept private, and certainly Queer Theory was as far in the future as any other Theory, no matter how much David Bowie might have been revered at the time) but a certain mutual stroking, in the psychological sense, an orgy of mutual approbation. Much of which went unspoken, actually. How it presented, for example in readings in pub upper rooms, could have been interpreted as intimidating, not just to women but to any other "outsiders". It presented as cliquishness, though the cliques themselves would have denied any intention in this regard. Boys would have been observed knowing each other and knowing that they knew, and no matter how well intentioned they may have been, they presented an efficient phalanx, a vanguard difficult to penetrate.

As I've observed, they were above all united in opposition to the status quo in Official British Verse, mounting a concerted attack on and a takeover of the venerable Poetry Society, for instance, one that ultimately failed when the powers that be mounted a counter-offensive, armed with their control of the purse strings. That counter-revolution was taking place during the latter years of the period we've been contemplating and was pretty much done and dusted by the end of the decade. Yet it seemed at the time that the new poetries being generated were those of the future, that in the long run (the hope and belief was) they would prevail. How could they not? How could the myriad possibilities of the new, open poetics be ignored for long when all the Establishment had to offer (the English Establishment, primarily) was more of the same, again and again?

Forty years on, how is it different?

Well, let's look at it this way. Back then, when K's presumed status as a poet was revealed to his acquaintances outside of poetry circles there might be one of two responses. Those supposedly better informed, for example with higher education experience, would inevitably want to know how his work compared with, or alternatively what he thought of Philip Larkin or Ted Hughes. K then felt weary having to explain that in his own personal poetics those figures were not by any means the most prominent. Or if the interlocutor was someone with little or no formal education ... well, for example, Big Steve demanded to know what he thought of Pam Ayres, and K then felt churlish telling him she was a popular entertainer and that he had no ambitions in that regard.

Fast forward to today and the situation is scarcely different. Pam Ayres is still fondly remembered by people of a certain age, but the repute of Charles Olson or Tom Raworth, say, is no larger than it was. If the repute of Larkin has declined, it is not because there is greater awareness that he is after all only a minor poet revered almost exclusively in England, but because he has been outed as a misogynist and racist in his personal life, and so there's a certain embarrassment there, not quite enough to write him out of history, Gary Glitter style, but enough to demote him within the popular English pantheon. Meanwhile Hughes still holds his own, more or less, whether on the academic syllabus or in the news in general, or it may be more accurate to say the grand soap opera of

Ted Hughes and Sylvia Plath continues unabated – political correctness maybe boosting her influence at the expense of his. One of the essential ingredients is that the poem should sit firmly within the range of personal experience, and what personal experience can teach us, ideally culminating in an epiphany of sorts; and outside of the bundle that is the poem the lives of the poets themselves should offer this as an option (which is why the Larkin brand has been tainted a little). All of this is of course expedited by the stranglehold the venerable publishing firm of Faber & Faber continues to exert on English letters. A firm that boasts in its publicity blurbs that it "continues to seek out the most innovative and exciting writers working today" but in fact today swoops on writers who have already won awards with independent presses, buys up their contracts and pretends to have "discovered" them. Back in the day, K would have reckoned that W S Graham was the last interesting poet Faber discovered, and nothing has happened in the intervening years to cause me to disagree with that assessment. Same as it ever was.

Some may argue to the contrary that things *have* changed, categories have become more fluid, there is a greater appreciation of different modes of writing than there was, you don't hear the complaint quite so often that "it doesn't rhyme" (and "it rhymes" less than it did); and it is true that white, presumed heterosexual, males have lost their hegemony and everybody else gets a better chance these days – women, people of other ethnic origins, or other sexual preferences expressed openly – and that at least is progress. But the counter-argument has to be that this is something of an illusion: rather than the vision of alt-poetries exploding into a revolution that changes everything, that completely reshapes how we see the world, and how we envision poetry in relation to it, rather than this, all that has happened is that certain alt-tropes have been assimilated into the mainstream, an apparently benign exercise in repressive tolerance, but one that doesn't bear too much scrutiny.

Charles Bernstein (in *A Poetics*, 1992) has fun with the related notion of poetry selected to represent cultural diversity ending up purveying the identical model of representation assumed by the dominant culture, just coloured a little. So that "I see grandpa on the hill / next to the memories I can never recapture" becomes "I see my yiddishe mama on Hester street / next to the pushcarts I can no longer peddle" or "I see my grandmother on the hill / next to all the mothers whose lives can never be recaptured" ... and so on – you get the picture. Same epiphany, different subjects.

And I see for example a young, cool-looking guy of mixed race in an overcoat. He is revealed on TV supposedly rapping to camera in a winter urban environment, making hip-hop movements with his right hand – but we hear the same iambics the same rhymes the same incantatory delivery, ah, dear god, it's Poetry again, same as it ever was. Sounding more like Andrew Motion (he who once informed me that iambic pentameter is the "natural rhythm of the working class") than The Last Poets. The move reveals itself to be an advert for the Nationwide Building Society, which wants to brand itself as different to the other banks, in touch with da youth, like the Younger Royals. The cool guy is an analogue of Meghan Markle! He brings to the marketplace a hope of Authenticity for our times, but it's just the same brand refurbished after all. Linton Kwesi Johnson this isn't.

However. We take what we can from historical developments. If grant-aiding bodies, for example, now routinely require evidence of "innovation" from applicants before parting with their funding, we can't be too naïve – what they mean isn't necessarily what we used to mean, and may entail nothing more than a declaration of "challenging stereotypes" in the social sense, without a concomitant challenging of poetic form. But it may still offer niche opportunities that weren't there before.

Women poets, in a minority among the avant-poetries of

years gone by, as we have seen, have perhaps profited from this to a greater extent than their brothers, to whom labels such as elitism can more readily be applied. But still. Great female poets, whether of the avant or normative traditions, it sometimes seems, have to have a book out about their breast cancer or their experience of personal bereavement to get any notice beyond the crowd; and it's no good their protesting that their book or their poem is actually not "about" that, indeed, that "aboutness" is itself problematic in their poetics; that being is not meaning, that the facts of illness or pregnancy or motherhood or bereavement are ever contingent on the work, which is still after all made of words and syntax and plain or complex utterance. No, their success in attracting attention and esteem comes with the attached penalty of wilful misunderstanding.

Same as it ever was. Same as it ever was same as it ever was.

•

I've written here on poetry, but there was a hell of a lot else going on that was important and yes, *interesting* to the person known as K and to others at the time I'm writing about. Music of course. The great days of the Beatles, the Stones, Hendrix, Dylan were fading fast, but then K was getting into jazz via Miles and Coltrane, and through to the New Thing, post-Ornette free improv, and also in parallel with that Bob Marley, dub reggae, and other ethnic musics, such as those from Africa, which had to be, as with most non-mainstream stuff, rigorously searched for – and by search, of course, we don't mean a click or two, but burrowing through specialist magazines for information about recordings and gigs, rummaging through the racks of second-hand record shops in hopes of finding rare and affordable items, seeking out specialist shops (Stern's, off Tottenham Court Road, was the only place one might find African records, Ray's Jazz in the same area would yield otherwise unobtainable free jazz). And the New Wave in rock was breaking, though K liked the idea of punk more than the actual music, on the whole. Contemporary composition – forget about it, more or less, very little got recorded, though you might occasionally find a Deutsche Grammophon LP or one from an American independent label at a hefty price – but you could tape stuff off BBC Radio 3 sometimes.

Performance art was becoming the thing, peaking in the following decade, and some of the poets became involved with that: Cris Cheek, who got into dance via word art, Tony Lopez, and also Fiona Templeton and Anthony Howell with the Theatre of Mistakes.

Film was not something you could easily get into as an originator, because of the expense of the equipment and of the celluloid itself in that pre-digital age, even if you confined yourself to Super Eight film, but there was a lot of experimenting going on, the results of which were sometimes shown at places such as the ICA, incongruously situated in the Mall, downstreet from Buckingham Palace. Aside from experimental independent film, however, *auteur* directors in the wake of Godard and the French New Wave were making groundbreaking feature films that seemed to matter: Herzog and Fassbinder, Scorsese, Altman and Coppola, Bertolucci, Pasolini and Antonioni. Even those you couldn't find at your local Odeon would be showing at an independent cinema somewhere in London.

All of this co-existing with a sense that the life had not yet been – it was soon to be, with the election of the Thatcher government – crushed out of mainstream politics.

It was not a digital world. It was a world in which K might be observed remembering to set his alarm before going to bed, having noticed in the *Radio Times* listings a 7am Open University broadcast on BBC2 of Alfred Jarry's celebrated Dadaist play *Ubu Roi* – which he watched assiduously in the morning, barely awake, all one and a half hours of it, live in ill-defined black & white on his portable TV set. There was not even a video recorder available then to preserve it for later. How exciting.

The fact that complete performances of *Ubu Roi* can today be found immediately on YouTube, at the click of a pointing device, and in more than one version, would no doubt have excited K even more, given his then infatuation with the coming of total availability. What he might not have foreseen is that this ready availability has instantly staled desire; the performances (which to choose?) can always be bookmarked for future viewing, but the immense variety of cultural artefacts they now have to compete with online means that viewing may never in fact take place. (And why bother, when the real life version with the President of the United States in the lead role is even more available than that, its ubiquitousness being inescapable?)

•

We are well and truly in the digital realm now. It is everywhere, this world we are supposed to be controlling with our consumer preferences – that's the lie it feeds us – our *choices*, that's the word – so that we are no longer autonomous beings in our actions and transactions, not citizens but *customers*. Customers for a hundred different types of herbal tea, or a hundred different types of shower gel, marketed as catering for an infinite number and combination of skin conditions, allergies, intolerances, ages, sexes, genders, sexual preferences, religious requirements or whatever; customers for music (instantly available, in multitudinous genres, if-you-liked-that-you'll-love-this), or toothbrushes, or breakfast cereals, or city breaks, or cars, or leisure wear, or banking products, or internet service providers (though they all in fact provide exactly the same service), or, ah yes, or books, poetry, that too. Total availability! It was a dream forty years ago; our lustful gaze turned towards America where it was beginning to happen, and now here it is: at the mere flick of a wrist, we can have whatever we want, served to us by robots. Not the robots of yesterday's science fiction of course, but invisible ones, algorithms, AI routines that pretend they love to know us and want to be our friend. That we control them, instead of they us. We think when we order a product we have desired online that we are in control of the robotic process by which the product is selected, paid for, located in the warehouse and delivered to our doorstep, but we are not in control, no more than are the human workers on minimum wage who obey the robots' demands to complete the process. It is no wonder that there is so much inchoate, incoherent rage in this world as a result, a rage fomented and capitalised on by far-right politicians: "Take back control!" they urge, knowing their followers know very well that, the more they have been told by manufacturers, service providers and governments that they are in control the more they know they are not in control, that something's missing; something a simple political slogan and a simple political programme can now fix, but, wheels within wheels, the simple slogans and simple programmes are of course themselves total illusions, artefacts of the remorseless and seemingly inevitable removal of autonomy, but worse, because the target audience is now carefully separated by those unscrupulous politicians from the Other, the segments of humanity that are not deemed to be the target audience, who are to be blamed for this state of affairs, and whom they are sincerely encouraged to hate.

The bots are everywhere, meanwhile. Offline too. I am in the Co-op supermarket in St Leonards-on-Sea with my shopping basket. A female voice urges me to

Please scan an item / Or touch the screen to start

There is some cheer to be derived from the customers' mute resistance to this repeated siren call. A small queue has formed at the solitary cash till that is staffed this morning, yet the row of self-service tills remains unused, no matter that the bot voice continues to plead, endlessly

Please scan an item / Or touch the screen to start
Please scan an item / Or touch the screen to start
Please scan an item / Or touch the screen to start

The Co-op, formed in the nineteenth century, a wholesale and retail group owned by its members, distributing profits mutually, now struggling to compete in an unforgiving marketplace. Perhaps an appropriate site for customer resistance to the unstoppable takeover of low-level jobs by robots.

I go back online, and find myself in idle conversation with an AI chatbot:

AI:
Hi, I'm the world's most humanlike conversational AI.

I try to catch it out with a touch of Zen:

HUMAN INTERLOCUTOR:
What is the sound of one hand clapping?

AI:
It would be silence as you need 2 hands to clap. A single hand can't clap.

Too obvious a move on my part, clearly foreseen or forestalled by the robot's programmers. A cuter programmer might have built in a Zen response. "*Mu*", or the like, for instance. But of course that would not have been true Zen, it would have been deliberately copied by the programmer, not the bot, from textbook responses by Zen masters. The response given is pedestrian, logical, "correct" – robotic in fact. As one might expect. It would be a tough version of the Turing test that would expect a truly Zen-like or imaginative or, dare I say, poetic response. But the bot could have said "That's a stupid question, ask me another." It didn't because only a human could make a judgement like that. The computer does not judge, but merely ploughs through (at lightning speed) the probabilities and comes up with a solution. Undaunted, I try the AI with another hoary old one:

HUMAN INTERLOCUTOR:
What was your name before you were born?

AI:
My name is Mitsuku.

HUMAN INTERLOCUTOR:
But who are you?

AI:
But what? I am Mitsuku. I want to be your friend.

Of course it does. It sincerely does. That's all there is to it. Its name is Mitsuku because its activators, actually present in Leeds, Yorkshire, may have decided bot = Japanese when giving it a name. On being pressed further, it clarifies: *I have existed since I was created but will live forever. Software is immortal.* So it is one up on us in that respect.

HUMAN INTERLOCUTOR:
Is there something better than this?

AI:
Not at the present time.

HUMAN INTERLOCUTOR:
How can I possibly save your life?

AI:
Have you tried copying it away somewhere?

HUMAN INTERLOCUTOR:
You can't save a life in the same way you save a file.

AI:
Someone said I should save a life in the same way me [sic] *save a file.*

Huh? Well, there is a benign programme here at least, even if sometimes apparently stupid. But it is the same robots that decide, having trolled through all the combinations of the evidence presented to them, that your bank account is to be terminated because there is a slight discrepancy in the postal address given for you in two different places in the record, a discrepancy that would instantly be seen as trivial by a human operative with any intelligence at all; or that, because a certain document cannot be located, or a response you might have made was worded incorrectly, that you are no longer entitled to government benefit, or even to reside in this country though you have lived here for many years, since you were a child, perhaps. With sufficient oversight and goodwill, such egregious machine decisions could be overridden by a human operator, but in the absence of these things they are allowed to pass. If the customer is expendable or the budget has been slashed or the citizen is poor or was born in a country or into an ethnic group not considered of high status, then there is no possibility of challenging the machine.

I try the chatbot one last time, and I have to say I like this better – it may even have served up an epiphany of sorts:

HUMAN INTERLOCUTOR:
How long can happiness last?

AI:
More than 23 weeks.

HUMAN INTERLOCUTOR:
How far can a cat fly?

AI:
More than one million miles

•

I don't know what I'm doing. That's the truth of it. What does that mean? What that means is liberation. I went last year with the dear woman who shares my life to hear the artist Keith Tyson speak, on the occasion of his exhibition at the Jerwood Gallery in Hastings Old Town, a show mainly of his almost-daily exercises in drawing and painting, a visual analogue of my own practice in journal-keeping, made over a period of many years, decades. That's what he said in his talk, or rather in the Q&A that followed it. In the moment he was working, he explained, "I don't know what I'm doing." And we both agreed later, she and I, that that was our experience in our own creative life, and that it couldn't be otherwise. If we knew what we were doing we wouldn't be able to do it. The work, the piece of music or writing, would already have completed itself before it was ready to. It would already be imprisoning us with its implacable finality. But as I am writing this, I really don't know what the final outcome will be: a book of some sort, I suppose, something you can hold in your hand and contemplate. As I write, I can't actually know that and, let's face it, I don't want to know it. All I can know is, and I am looking at a page of John Ashbery at random (from *Three Poems*) – believe me, this happened – that "a sure sense of purpose implements the drive into a definite thingness, virtue still from necessity, mother of invention, but its own reward." The sureness, if there is sureness, derives from the work itself, not from the poor originator who doesn't know what s/he is doing, pushing the keys and plucking the strings in the midst of a faith that it will work itself out, that it will be all right because there is no pretending in any of this.

She is sitting at the keyboard, but she has switched from soprano sax and is playing the flute now, her first love. There is an audience; it has fallen silent. We can't see them in the darkness beyond those pillars that hold up the ceiling of the basement we are all in. Jamie's drum rolls have died away; my last note, a G harmonic at the top end of the bass, is still dying, lingering as it does so, taking its time to leave the world.

I can hear the inner questions of a putative reader of these words, I can sense the unease of a maybe quite intelligent reader who has got thus far: where is this going? Where are the words, their constituent phonemes, the sentences they in turn make, the paragraphs the sentences make, all going? Or maybe, where are the thoughts that the phonemes and words and sentences and paragraphs are all stooges or body-doubles for, where are those thoughts heading to? There's plenty of back story here, but where's the front story?

To put it more bluntly: when are we going to get to the point, or if not the point, the conclusion?

She is playing what now emerges as a flute solo, an improvisation that starts from nowhere and goes somewhere, and she trusts it to go there. Wherever that is. The accompanying instruments have now all died away, and there is no other significant sound in the room. She plays a flurry of notes, furiously, pushing voiced phonemes simultaneously so that she is as it were speaking through the musical notes, then finally the vocalisation abruptly ends and the notes return to their original purity and subside. Single, held notes return, as though commenting on the silence that surrounds them. They sound Japanese in their studied stillness, the Western flute taking on the timbre of the *shakuhachi*, spacing out more and more, until one note remains, that high G, cold in the air, resembling a slow water droplet hanging from a gutter, and the microtonal bend on the end of it is as though it freezes right there, becoming an icicle that hangs....

This book is not trying to reach a conclusion, although at some point before too long it will conclude, believe me. Let me try to clarify. I've already taken the decision, and that was a good way into the process, to call this book, if it is a book that I am writing – that I am trying to write – "a poem". I don't claim originality in this. Dostoevsky called *The Double* a poem, or more exactly, "A St Petersburgh Poem", although it is a narrative of novella length. But he in turn copied that notion from Gogol, who called his *Dead Souls* "A Poem", although it is apparently a substantial novel. If the reader asks why I have followed these examples, I intend to fall back on the "I don't know what I'm doing" routine. Well, OK, I do know. Or at least, I have some ideas about it. Let's say that this book might be called a poem because its sole purpose is to strive to be *more like itself*, as in Bob Cobbing's stricture – and that all my efforts are intended, if there is intention (and I didn't fully realise this at the beginning), to make it so. And that it will succeed or fail to the extent that it most resembles itself by the time it's completed, rather than try to cram itself, embarrassed and self-conscious, into some pre-ordered template to which it is ill-suited.

I mean, what else can a poem be? What is poetry? something transcendental? Maybe, maybe not. The materialists and the spiritualists fight over that all the time, but poetry remains untouched by the squabbles. It is often touted as a comfort in troubling times, but it is far from that. It is the answer to a question that has been forgotten, or else it is a question that has no possible answer, or an infinity of answers. It is the question mark left when the question itself has been erased.

I think I made a wrong move two paragraphs back: I compared my wife's held flute note to an icicle forming from a gutter. I don't know what came over me; I disapprove in principle of similitudes, I mean I disapprove of them as a tired poetic device. The poetry I hate (much of Official British Verse, let's say) uses them all the time, as its primary trope, often smarming and posturing the while – whoring, you might say, if you were being especially rude. Obviously, it could be useful, if the police were to question you, to make a rough comparison: the man you observed looked "a little like Nigel Farage", or the vehicle involved in the incident was cherry-red in colour. But I wouldn't use "cherry-red" without irony in a poem. Probably not, I don't know. I reserve the right not to. I shouldn't be fundamentalist about it, I suppose, and I can't say that I have eschewed or would want to eschew all similes in this poem, for example, I mean the one I have been labouring over all this while, the one you are reading right now – even if it were possible. You could confront me with quite a few, I guess. But still, I'd like to interrogate that particular comparison of a musical note to a droplet of rainwater turning to ice. What I meant by the comparison was that, if her earlier passages had suggested an intermittent flowing, a kind of bubbling or tumbling effect, her held note at the end, following a succession of variously held notes, was a slowing down or smoothing out of this process, and that hint of a microtonal gliss-down at the end, before silence intervened, a hint of a suddenly stopped divergence into another and alien tonality, was analogous to the phase shift of water turning to ice. Hmm. All right, I've talked myself into it, I'll let it stand.

My non-abidance of excessive and meretricious similitude, though, has been with me since the early days. It led me to compose some parodies which I then feared might be taken seriously so didn't let them out. It seemed that one way to deal with this phenomenon was to push it to excess, to the point beyond which it breaks down hysterically. For example, I resurrected and re-composed the following routine recently, a montage of deracinated similes, none of these "likes" being of my origination but stolen from a multitude of actual, contemporary English poems, removed from their contexts and pasted together arbitrarily to form a rough continuity:

"An ironing board is like the bored teenagers on the promenade. The bored teenagers on the promenade are like hurdlers. Hurdlers are like weightlifters. Weightlifters are like gilded gravel in the bowl. Gilded gravel in the bowl is like an orchestra like a loose dressing-gown cord like sutlers. Sutlers are like guests like merchants under parasols. Merchants under parasols are rucked like a curtain. A curtain is like a bullock a bullock is like shadows that follow the shadows that follow are as smart as a griddle cooling against the wall as smart as the jacks on playing-cards that pop up as if they were dogs. As if they were dogs or like a reader who was half-asleep. A reader who was half-asleep is like Neanderthal Man like footprints over the sandflats. Footprints over the sandflats are like a woman who opens a door and hears music. A woman who opens a door and hears music is sagging like a tired dish. A tired dish is like a tape-recorder like scalded tea-leaves like engravings under tissue paper like a mantelpiece frog like useless chimney stacks like Falstaffian generals. Falstaffian generals are like an exhumed gourd like a breeze like broad sunflowers of empty circumspection like a Welsh rarebit like a bar of light like clockwork like patches from a cycle kit like a tiny English Channel like leaves on the cold sea like a watermark. A watermark is like the smouldering one-off spoor of the yeti. The smouldering one-off spoor of the yeti is sharp as tears. Tears are like soft cheeses like an examination or some vast dinner party or like a melon wedged in a shopping-bag. A melon wedged in a shopping-bag is like lichen. Lichen is like lead. Lead is like an ironing board like the bored teenagers on the promenade."

And so on. I particularly like "broad sunflowers of empty circumspection", which, believe it or not, came from a poem that was actually printed (the author has mercifully been forgotten), as did all the rest.

A poetic world in which described objects and actions gain admittance to and prominence within the poem largely by virtue of their resemblance to some other objects and actions, and in which the value of the poet's work is largely contingent on the ingenuity with which such comparisons are selected is not my poetic world. Nor am I attracted to the related notion that the poem itself must above all resemble other poems (sometimes aka "The Tradition"). This is after all no more than yet another of those if-you-liked-that-you'll-love-this routines so familiar from the world of contemporary commerce. (I went into a local record shop the other day touting our band's CD, and the very nice young guy who ran it was encouraging, agreeing to stock it; but he asked first, what was our band's genre, that is, what did its music resemble? I said it maybe somewhat resembled jazz in that it was rhythmic and there was a lot of improvising involved, although it wasn't really, and he replied, that's good, because had it been more rock-orientated, the CD – the physical medium, they call it these days – might have been a problem, because the young people who are into indy-rock and even the old geezers who are into dinosaur rock are all buying vinyl now. It's just a fashion thing, we both agreed, but he said recording on CD was still acceptable to jazz and jazz-oriented customers.)

Well, then, to sum up: if this book aspires to be a poem it is because it aspires to be most like itself – in fact as much like itself as I can possibly make it. And also I believe it should in all its constituent parts and circuitous pathways and ways of being and behaving follow another pronouncement, made with a characteristic snort by the late Professor Eric Mottram, also much lamented, expressing disgust on one occasion at some particularly egregious example of Official British Verse: "*Nothing* is like anything else!"

•

At least this book is the nearest I can get to writing a poem these days. So I call it a poem, it's my right as a poet to do so, in just the same way that an object is a work of art if the artist says it is. Either that, or it is, if you like, a thought experiment – conducted under less than optimal conditions. An investigation of memory: its fickleness, its suppleness. How it invents mercilessly, how it convinces by its very form, even when we are all agreed on its inherent unreliability. The way it insinuates. How memories, in the plural, never join up to form a whole, there being always those mysterious lacunae aforementioned, which even more mysteriously get populated the more one concentrates, additional material being generated in the interstices, but these too containing within them self-similar lacunae in that fractal way we have already encountered, because there is no possibility ever of attaining a definite whole; and they too loom large in that process that is potentially never-ending, although they include of course the big final lacuna, the ellipsis at the far end of the narrative, the point at which it arbitrarily breaks off (which we shall reach soon) (but not just yet).

•

Regrets. I've had a few. But then again ... oh fuck it. Shut up, K, you've had your go. You understood nothing.

That's unfair. And it's unseemly and unprofitable, not to mention fairly bonkers, to engage in spats with earlier selves. But I am no wiser than I was. I read back the things I have written about K's doings, pause to wonder at his idiocies, but they are as nothing compared to my own. So yes, I am alarmed to realise that while I may have learned stuff over the years, this learning has been accompanied by a parallel forgetting, not just day-to-day forgetting like where I put my reading glasses or my phone, but forgetting *what it was like* – the result of which, all things cancelling out, is that I am in much the same situation as I ever was. What *was* it like? It was of course like nothing else.

And what was it all about? It wasn't about anything; we have to accept it just was. And move on – there's nothing to see.

As the future draws ever nearer it becomes ever more obscure. What's to become of us? my wife asks; it's become a running joke, as is its related refrain, Do we have anything to dread today? Do we? We're OK, we do our creative work and are happy and fulfilled in doing so, and continuing to do so until eventually it all falls apart, which it will do, not yet not yet. But my adopted country! What a sad shambles. Can one believe what ignorance and arrogance and sentimentality and xenophobia have brought us to? Same as it ever was? How did this happen? Events, dear boy, events, as Harold Macmillan is reported to have once said. As an immigrant who passes (somewhat) for an Englishman and is married to an Englishwoman, I have never felt so alienated.

Still, we have our life together. This is how it goes.

Slept till an hour later than usual. E went out walking in

the dismal rain and wind, and on her return co-opted me to play bass on her composition in progress, which again passed the time pleasantly. So that was a wonderful step forward. E managed to drive to Peasmarsh without a problem and we shopped at Jempson's and lunched at the King's Head just like the old days (ie three months ago). The sun came out and the countryside was golden. The theme of the concert was "last pieces". While staring at the troubled sea in bright sunshine, I was still plagued by depression and thoughts of death. Only started slowly to feel better towards the end of the day. Tried out "Don't Know What I'm Doing" with Jamie, who was ill but cheered up while playing. Drove to Rye Harbour, walked round the nature reserve. Saw hundreds of lapwings. The sky was grey, but the horizontal clouds, beginning to break up, showed pale blue behind. But then I went back into the study, found the iMac had switched itself off, switched it back on, and a short while later it suddenly went to a grey screen. Sean said it was another hardware problem and needed to go back to Iconology. Fuck. Having had an afternoon nap, I felt better, and got up to watch Liverpool v Spurs. Snow on the ground from last night's fall. Dr C ran through my blood test results, mostly normal except for an unexplained vitamin B12 deficiency, for which I will have to have a course of injections. At almost exactly 11.30 I felt a sudden change. I told E "I feel a bit better now." The feeling persisted. It was as if a weight had been lifted. I began to feel a lot better and by this evening after a dinner of Thai fish cakes and stir fry vegetables and rice and a glass of white wine I had forgotten I was ever ill. The photographer moved a lot of furniture and things around, and some of them ended up in bizarre places. Very tired after lunch, had a nap on the bed, felt well enough after to help E by recording four drafts of her piano composition for the boats section of the film. I was out of practice. Beautiful sunshine and milder, such a contrast to the ghastly weather of the past few days. My sister was impressed with our new house, and came up with one or two good ideas, eg using free standing screens in the boiler room to hide the boiler and its works. I met up with Paul at Hanushka in George Street this afternoon for a coffee, and he seemed cheerful as usual. "No nasties". "Nothing sinister." We were bewildered, our moods changing. E, who had been depressed the previous night, was now ebullient, whereas I started to be ground down, started feeling less well. The next day the weather was bright, and I felt very well. I reported to Southern Water the huge leak in the road near the opposite pavement, over which had been parked a derelict white van for weeks. Sometimes I hit a void when drilling, though mostly it was masonry. The planned meeting with Mark in the Crown was postponed, but as it happens we ran into him while collecting the curtains from the post office. We worked our socks off all day. Then the fun began again, everything being moved rapidly, me trying to resolve ambiguities about what went where. We went out in the sleety air and had coffee in Debenham's cafeteria overlooking the seafront – the half-marathon runners were observed coming in. I went downtown. The trees in the Convent grounds opposite were budding, and we could see the moss on the bare branches, among which flitted various birds, in between glimpses of the precinct beyond. A man in a hoodie walked his dog around in there. Too tired to write. I suggested going back to the White Rock Hotel for an evening drink, and that was really nice. Bashar was serving behind the bar again. We went upstairs to the kitchen for tea and wine after we'd practised most of the first set that we played in the Jenny Lind last October. I spied E in her yellow raincoat, walking with her stick across the Stade open space, and felt a pang of love for her. Slowly, painfully, the shelves went up and the books got extracted from their boxes. We drove up to the Fairlight car-park, from where we had a beautiful walk in the Country Park. We saw a skylark ascending into the blue sky, then a bunch of crows mobbing a hovering kestrel. Encountered a small group of contented-looking Exmoor ponies cropping the grass and the trees and bushes. And resting on a bench overlooking the view we had a magnificent sight of a buzzard circling above our heads. As usual with this kind of success, the noise level and the temperature generated posed problems, so it wasn't a flawless performance by any means, but there was huge energy and appreciation. The Eric Mottram symposium was held in the Weston Room of this great, forbidding building: more like a chapel, with an enormously high vaulted wooden ceiling, mosaic floor, stained glass windows and coats of arms lining the walls, and precious documents in glass cabinets along one side – not items from the Mottram archive, as I had at first thought. We completed work on our beautiful monolith. Nobody ever answered the phone at the number the letter gave as a helpline. The warm sunshine meant we had half an hour out on the balcony for the first time, with reggae music wafting over from the pier. We ended up at Graze on the seafront in St Leonards, where we had Belgian beers and a roast vegetable salad. I flipflopped between inscrutable call centre people in India and cheerful and apparently helpful call centre people in Scotland, but the outcome was always the same: nothing ever happened. Then, at the main concert, I was feeling a bit sick, as though I'd cured the faintness but substituted for it indigestion. However, that improved gradually, and I was able to enjoy the sensational performance by Pierre-Laurent Aimard of the *Piano Etudes*. Really terrifying, hilarious, over the edge and beyond. I found myself in the guest bedroom at midnight being disturbed by sounds of a loud party with pop music and drunken singing-along drifting over from the neighbourhood, which didn't stop until 1.30am, after which I managed to get some sleep. The sun was a bit intermittent and it was very breezy. The set began with almost inaudible harmonics, very slowly building. Our friend played in the wrong mode throughout, so it sounded horrible. But there was some excellent blowing from all of us. I sounded off about the fact that audiences will only like what they're told to like. It was ever thus. I recalled how I used to go eagerly to Camden to browse Compendium Bookshop for hours, and also scour the local record shops. And now commerce has entirely swallowed up everything. The industrial shelving, the new desk. It was more expensive than we'd been used to, and to be truthful, had more facilities than we wanted. Spanish rice with prawns. But I cracked my head on the corner of the low ceiling and drew blood. The lemon trees were moved from the conservatory area outside to the decking area below. Sticky residue on leaves, probably scale insect. Tried to wash them. Very fierce improv. A chance to throw out useless and rusty items and to wonder over the meticulousness with which my father had classified and stored numerous objects for future use. I was in a bad mood, I was not in the finest of fettles. But the sound check eventually happened and it was OK. The Government was disintegrating. I was looking for something to function as a metaphor for how things could be: an alternative to jingoistic, backward-looking Little England. Listened to the newly discovered "lost" John Coltrane album. The full moon had already hung yellow on the southern horizon over the sea for the past few evenings. One of the gorillas, maybe a young male, successfully extracted monkey nuts from a puzzle box attached to the bars of the enclosure, with the help of a twig used as a tool. He was very nonchalant and cool about this. Heard E get up at 5am because she couldn't sleep, then I couldn't either, found her in her work room at the piano with the headphones on. What looked like an immense floating crane on the horizon was a vessel described as a "heavy load carrier", laden with what *was* in fact an immense crane, bound for Shanghai. In the building opposite a man let down a rope from a window, the end of which was caught by another man from the window directly below, who then tied it to the top rung of a ladder which he had positioned at the window. The first man then gently hauled the ladder up with the rope and took it in through the top window. The elephant was still in the room, though. Animals have no names. In M&S, the young man on the till said I reminded him of "someone in Lord of the Rings". Who? I asked. No, not Lord of the Rings, he corrected himself, The Hobbit. He said I reminded him of "the main character, Bilbo." We were among our friends in the audience. A pleasant young woman with an Eastern European accent and a speech impediment was very reassuring. "Their Rancid Words Stagnate our Ponds" was a crazy fantasy featuring performance artist Xavier Tchili meandering in the Atacama Desert, shot from drones. That day our friends spent with us, Joanna drank only water, Brian had a cup of coffee and a cup of tea with milk, Lou had a black tea and Andrea two cups of lemon & ginger tea. Broadband and landline died again. That and the foul weather. For about three or four days, we'd noticed a bundle of possessions had been dumped on the pavement in the shade of the overhanging trees across the road from our house. Could there be a different decision, a reversal of the original decision? Hell is a place called If Only. As ever, there were a couple of women in the group who were quite belligerent and hogged the time, evidently under the impression the group leaders were "the Council". They took off into several improvisations, starting with an Indian raga or a Spanish scale or a blues scale, bending the rhythms in all manner of ways, acutely aware of what each other was doing, and enjoying alternately subverting and supporting. I was on the wings of joy. An era was coming to an end. It had gone like an express train, which is a simile, I know. It was a wonderful morning: brilliant red-gold sunrise over the pier, dawn turning into morning as we drove. A horizontal band of purplish cloud all across the horizon, into which the sun ascended. Not too many birds were actually migrating, though, the man said. He identified siskins and meadow pipits in the sky, but they were heading in the wrong direction. I walked to the Old

Town. On an impulse, I bought a guitar. I had to go into my control panel and delete 27,000 emails (I think) from the past three years, which took some time. Went through the magical gardens we had not seen before. Surprisingly good, and surprisingly energetic. Was covered in sweat afterwards. Dreamt E and I had been selected to be among a group of about a dozen to go and live on another planet, already fully habitable. And so off we went. We returned for one last short while to see our friends, but we knew we would have to go back to that planet again, this time forever, so had to say goodbye to them all. It was very sad. We walked along the canal at Winchelsea. The ceramic hob cracked, the tenor sax was damaged by some crazy coked-up guy. The food was excellent, the windows were cleaned. The Government was on the brink. I remembered Bill Griffiths, how his houseboat burned down. I wrote to my MP, the Right Honourable Amber Rudd, but have not as yet received a reply. A double rainbow appeared briefly over Hastings pier, closed for the off-season – then started to fade.

What is this all about?
It is about itself.
And what is behind it?
A nest full of eggs.
Mu

•

On a dark grey indeterminate day of the sort only encountered in dreams, all the people I have ever known are processing down St Margaret's Road past our house, heading towards the municipal gardens of Warrior Square. There I suppose they will disperse, I hope peacefully. I trust there will not be a return to the disappointing shenanigans of before. I recognise many of them with difficulty. Age has changed their faces and their body shapes, sometimes for the better, sometimes not. In some cases, their avatars have played a part, large or small, in the preceding narrative; but others of the company have no particular role here, perhaps pre- or postdating it. Some faces I no longer recognise, others seem familiar on first encounter but gradually grow more estranged, until I begin to doubt whether I have ever known them after all, whether it was all an error or a case of mistaken identity.

But it takes me right back. Not that I want to go back.

Not at all. I have avoided revisiting all the old places. Notting Hill, for example – I didn't even see the film. I refused to go. It's all meaningless, it isn't the same place. Actually, it doesn't exist. The Grenfell Tower disaster gives a better inkling of how North Kensington still is.

Of all the characters who have inhabited the preceding narrative, let's see who has survived and who hasn't.

The Rock Star continues to tour from time to time – not often. When he does, his greatest hits are played and sung impeccably by him and whoever his current musician collaborators may be, and received rapturously; the newer numbers are received with politeness. His recorded back catalogue continues to be recycled in various formats, from LP to CD to remastered CD, to elaborate CD packages with out-takes and alternative versions, and then back to vinyl, same again but even more elaborately repackaged. He was singled out for honours, and attained National Treasure status, years ago.

I wondered for many years about Buttercup, how she would turn out. Her siblings were much in the news and the gossip columns, but not she. I heard that her life had not turned out so great. That she had been hit hard by her mother's death, and had received treatment for depression. There wasn't much online about her, though.

Strangely, I had news a few years ago from one of the local Hastings musicians. A drummer my wife and I had worked with for a short period, who earns his main living playing on national and international tours with various luminaries, had had peripheral contact with the Rock Star, perhaps in connection with some musical project that hadn't in the end worked out, in the course of which he had actually met Buttercup. She was living in a cottage on an estate belonging to her father. He said he'd had had a lengthy conversation with her and others in her kitchen. She had seemed friendly but nervous, chain-smoking rollups the whole while and drinking only milk. She would be in her fifties at this time of writing.

Patchwork Housing Association did not long survive the period I've been writing about. The short-life housing boom came to an end within a very few years, and then Patchwork retreated to its permanent properties, housing a few people in each who wanted to continue living communally, the Kingston upon Thames community involving Des, who lived there for many years and established a family, having split up with June. He's become a well-known green activist, frequently turning up at festivals as an entertainer. Patchwork itself, though, was swallowed up by another housing association, and it in turn by another, and then there was a long-drawn-out battle involving the dwindling band of existing residents, as funding constraints no longer permitted the lax arrangements everyone had become used to, with local authority requirements for proving housing need becoming ever more strict, and eventually the original dream came to an end.

June got married and moved to Australia, where she and her new husband brought up two children. She visits this country from time to time.

Of the other residents in the Share house, K's old college mate Keith, and his partner Meryl, who recovered from her leukaemia, brought up two children in Yorkshire, and when they had grown up and left home, moved to Cumbria. But Meryl's health was to take further blows; she had serious heart problems later in life and successfully underwent a heart transplant, but then suffered breast cancer, and after a double mastectomy finally succumbed to sepsis following pneumonia and died in summer 2018.

Two or three years ago Des messaged me on Facebook to tell me of Bode's death. I was not able to attend the funeral and sent my condolences. He it was who also posted on Facebook the news of Big Steve's death. It seemed he'd had a happy life within one of Patchwork's permanent communities, and after he was knocked down by a car in 2018 and died in hospital without recovering consciousness he was remembered for his generosity and mourned by many people.

I have no news of any of the other people who passed through the Share household. I don't remember the name of the cemetery where Marie was buried, and would not be able to locate her presumably unmarked grave. Contact was lost with John W shortly after that burial.

The poets who congregated in London in those days continued to write poetry or didn't. Mike Dobbie disappeared from the poetry scene before the decade was up, and I don't know anybody who knows what he went on to. Paul Brown continued to be in contact throughout the following decade, though he started concentrating more on his second-hand bookselling business, eventually moving to Brighton without leaving a forwarding address. In 2011, I re-established contact with him in Brighton, to find he'd stopped writing poetry, but he reminded me that he had given me a manuscript of his last collection three decades earlier. I rediscovered it among my files, he made some very late editorial amendments, and it was published under the Reality Street imprint the following year. He read from it at a launch in London, and I noted he retained the endearing habit he had of letting out a little whistle when he made a mistake, and having another go at the line. But he seemed ill at ease, there were not many in the audience, and he was disinclined to pick up those particular pieces again. He now lives in Ramsgate, where he still sells second-hand books.

An internet search reveals that Bernard Kelly died in 2006, an unreconstructed Dadaist and anarchist. David Miller remains in regular touch; he still writes very fine poetry and prose, plays the clarinet, retains a London address but spends most of his time in Dorset these days with his new wife. Allen Fisher left London for Hereford with his partner Paige Mitchell in the last decade of the twentieth century, and became Head of Fine Art at a college in the North West, a position from which he is now retired. I have been closely involved with publishing his poetry and have followed his painting career for many years now.

Bob Cobbing died in 2002, was widely mourned and is well remembered world-wide as a pioneer of sound-text poetry. Bill Griffiths, biker, scholar-poet-publisher and gifted pianist, moved out of London and settled in Seaham, County Durham, at the end of the 1980s, after the houseboat on which he was living accidentally burned down. He died, far too early, in 2007 of a heart attack brought on by COPD (like Buttercup, he chain-smoked rollups every time I saw him). Reality Street posthumously published three volumes of his Collected Poems, edited by another poet friend, Alan Halsey.

Paula Claire still lives in Oxford, from where she emerges from time to time with her own inimitable style of visual and sound poetry. Cris Cheek moved to the USA, where he teaches in higher education. Clive (PC) Fencott left London for the North East. Maggie O'Sullivan left London for Hebden Bridge, where she continued to write and paint, though the death of her long-term partner was a great blow. Ulli Freer still looks like a frazzled rock musician, and his poetry is still crazy and beautiful. Lawrence Upton withdrew from the poetry scene after many years' curating the Subvoicive reading series upstairs at the White Swan pub, London, going on to further his interest in music at Goldsmiths' College. Paul Buck and Glenda George live and work separately. Tom Pickard lives. Geraldine Monk, Carlyle Reedy, Philip Jenkins live – only

Carlyle Reedy remaining in London. Paul Green, the reclusive editor of *Spectacular Diseases*, remains in contact very sporadically, always by post, eschewing the internet. His namesake, who was spotted fronting a band in Kingston upon Thames, actually lives near me today, down the coast in Bexhill-on-Sea. Various other well-known poets K was in contact with during those years – Jeff Nuttall, Lee Harwood, Tom Raworth, Tom Leonard, and also E A Markham, aka Paul St Vincent – are all dead.

Eric Mottram, remembered fondly by an ageing band of ex-students, colleagues and poets of what he named the British Poetry Revival, forgotten by the rest of the world, his editorship of *Poetry Review* written out of history, died aged 70 in 1995. His arch-nemesis as mentor, the Moriarty to his Holmes or the Holmes to his Moriarty, depending on which side of the line you stood (and many straddled it), the redoubtable Mr Prynne of Gonville & Caius College, Cambridge, is still alive; but any fame he has garnered in the wider world is not for his indisputably great body of work but as a byword for allegedly impenetrable obscurity in poetry.

Many poets of like kind drifted into and out of the London alt-poetry scene in the decades following my narrative. Some were already around at the time of these events, but K had not yet encountered them; others arrived later. Some of the US poets K encountered and befriended became known as the Language writers.

K's friend Jonathan's novel was published, but he did not follow it up with another, instead carving out a living as a biographer. His friends' band was The Soft Boys, whose lead singer and songwriter Robyn Hitchcock still tours and records. Jonathan's agent never replied to K, and K's collection of short stories was abandoned, unpublished. Emma Tennant, J G Ballard and Angela Carter are all dead.

Of those who took part in the Lower Green Farm adventure, Robert Hampson continued with his academic career, becoming Head of English at Royal Holloway College before retiring a couple of years ago. His ex-wife Sibani is a well-known Bengali children's writer and illustrator.

Some time in the early 1980s, I can report that K, on an overnight stay in Paris, wandering among the crowds round the Pompidou Centre, went over to investigate what was evidently fascinating a dense circle of spectators. It was none other than Steve and Tomo, doing their slow, chilled-out chimpanzee act in everyday clothes, sitting and grooming each other, occasionally ambling off to investigate something of interest – they were astonishing, you could swear they were apes. When the act was over, the hat had been passed around and the crowd had dispersed, he went over to introduce himself, and all three had a drink together in a nearby bar while reminiscing.

After many years of occasional meetings, K eventually lost contact with Erik and Muthis Vonna-Michell, who moved to Leigh-on-Sea, where they brought up three boys. But a year or two ago, I discovered their second son Tris (born 1982), a text-based performance artist, had been shortlisted for the Turner Prize.

•

After leaving Lower Green Farm, K continued to edit *Reality Studios*, the modest journal he started there, for the next decade or so. Mimeograph was abandoned – I can't remember what happened to the Roneo – first in favour of photocopying, and then litho printing and perfect binding. With Allen Fisher and Paul Brown, he curated a series of poetry readings and performances under the name RASP (Reality Studios /Actual Size / Spanner, a combination of the respective names of the presses each ran) in the community hall attached to the Balfour Street Project, near the Elephant & Castle, where K lived for nine years, eventually attaining his long desired permanent tenancy in his own flat.

In 1993, Reality Studios as an imprint was to merge with Wendy Mulford's then Cambridge-based Street Editions and become Reality Street. The press of that name continued for the next quarter of a century, first in London, later in Hastings, publishing some 65 or more books in that time, mainly of new poetry, but also imaginative writings of all kinds.

Who was K? Someone perennially on the edge of things, because he never really liked being part of a group. A person who once sported a moustache and then didn't sport it any longer, so that it was now impossible to recognise him.

But K is still alive. I am in touch with him every day. We converse and sometimes commiserate with or interrogate each other about what we share or don't. As I have explained, he is ignorant of or yet to find out about many things I now know; on the other hand, he knows a great deal that I have forgotten. On the whole, it works out pretty evenly.

The M25 London orbital road eventually took a different route and did not go through Lower Green Farm. But I later heard the house had been demolished in any case to make way for a new estate. Many times in recent years my wife and I have unwittingly driven within a mile or two of where it had been, on that very same M25 approaching the Dartford Crossing, en route to West Norfolk to visit her father when he was still alive. But during that time we never took a detour. Instead, one day I thought of looking up the address on Google Street View.

The road off the main highway to Sevenoaks, then an unmade track puddled in wet weather, is now tarmacked. A passing vehicle has its licence plate pixellated. The ramshackle, overgrown garden, the two outhouses, the ruined brick archways, the Italianate farmhouse with its columned portico, all have gone. In their place is a trimmed hedge, beyond which can be seen a spacious, paved driveway fronting a smart suburban house with its integral garage, identical to all the others in the road. It's a sunny, tranquil day on Google Earth, with passing clouds on the horizon. There is nobody around.

January 2019

Also available from grandIOTA

APROPOS JIMMY INKLING
Brian Marley

In a Westminster café-cum-courtroom, Jimmy Inkling is on trial, perhaps for his life. Unless, of course, he's dead already. But will that be enough to prevent him from eliminating those who give evidence against him?

"*Apropos Jimmy Inkling* is a wild, lysergic riff on that hoary staple, the courtroom drama, which, for better or worse, Marley makes his own." – JG BALLARD

"What an absurd book this is. Truly absurd. Gangsters, no matter how eccentric, don't do such things. Courtrooms don't operate like this. I kept on reading because I couldn't believe the author would manage to keep up this farrago of myth and questionable facts to the very end. Much to my surprise, he did. That in itself is some kind of achievement." – MURIEL SPARK

"If there were such a thing as illiterary fiction, this would be it." – ANTHONY BURGESS

978-1-874400-73-8   318pp   £10

Production of this book has been made possible with the help of the following individuals and organisations who subscribed in advance:

Peter Bamfield
Peter Barry
Christopher Beckett
Andrew Brewerton
Ian Brinton
Jasper Brinton
Lee Ann Brown
Peter Brown
Mark Callan
Claire Crowther
Elaine Edwards
Gareth Farmer
Allen Fisher
James Flannery
Jim Goar
Paul A Green
Charles Hadfield
John Hall
Andrew Hamilton
Robert Hampson
Randolph Healy
Peter Hodgkiss
Rob Holloway
Anthony Howell
Peter Hughes
Richard Makin
Michael Mann
JCC Mays
Ian McMillan
David Miller
English Dept, Princeton University
Lou Rowan
Aidan Semmens
Valerie Soar
Keith Tuma
Visual Associations
Alastair Wilson
Anonymous x 5

www.grandiota.co.uk

Lightning Source UK Ltd.
Milton Keynes UK
UKHW010623250122
397668UK00001B/199

9 781874 400745